Endorsements

"In *25,000 Mornings* Rowe writes with characteristic freshness and charm, framing her thoughts with penetrating clarity and spiritual perceptiveness, and yet with a hint of playfulness that engages the reader." Rev. Peter Black, author *Parables from the Pond*

"Fay Rowe offers readers another compelling book packed with wisdom. Wrapped in warm humor, Rowe's book encourages in a world where we all need encouragement. *25,000 Mornings* draws us step-by-step closer to God and leaves us feeling prepared to face the day." Donna Fawcett, award-winning author of the Donna Dawson novels; writing instructor, Fanshawe College, London, Ontario

"Fay Rowe continues to delight with honesty and humor. As she scrutinizes God's Word and openly shares the times when she has to refocus her own thoughts on the heart of the Father, she gently stirs the reader to do likewise." Mary Haskett, award-winning author of *Reverend Mother's Daughter* and *Because We Prayed*

Also by Fay Rowe

Smooth Stones and Promises

Keepers of the Testimony

25,000 MORNINGS

Ancient Wisdom for a Modern Life

F A Y   R O W E

WESTBOW
P R E S S
A DIVISION OF THOMAS NELSON

All scriptures, unless otherwise noted, are from The Authorized King James
Version, The World Publishing Company, Cleveland and New York, 1945

WestBow Press books may be ordered through booksellers or by contacting:

WestBow Press
A Division of Thomas Nelson
1663 Liberty Drive
Bloomington, IN 47403
www.westbowpress.com
1-(866) 928-1240

ISBN: 978-1-4497-3369-8 (sc)
ISBN: 978-1-4497-3368-1 (e)
Library of Congress Control Number: 2011962127

Printed in the United States of America

WestBow Press rev. date: 1/18/2012

TO GLENN

My partner in everything.

PREFACE

Dear Friend,

A few years ago, a television ad for the state of Michigan said we have 25,000 mornings, give or take a few. Michigan has given us 68.49 years—no doubt an average based on the recorded life spans of both the good and the evil.

I'm very sure God has given us more time than has the state of Michigan!

I've lived a considerable number of mornings already, and I've learned a few things about life. One of the most important things I've learned about life is this: We need God in it.

One way to ensure we keep God in our lives is to keep him in our days. I'm convinced that as we start each day by turning our thoughts to him and his ways it will help us live our very best life, and our thousands of days will be filled with his goodness.

As we spend the next few mornings together, I hope these simple devotional offerings help you begin your morning with a sense of joy and peace, and with expectation for what God has for you—and has for you to do—in the rest of your day.

God bless you!

Fay

"For I am not ashamed of the gospel of Christ: for it is the power of God unto
salvation to everyone that believeth"
(Romans 1:16)

ON STARTING OUT, OR STARTING OVER

There's excitement in it, and anxiety.

In either case, it is an affirmation of life.

25,000 Mornings

God said he's given us *all things richly to enjoy*, didn't he?

If every new morning truly is from him, filled with his mercy and loving kindness, then deciding to enjoy each one sounds like wisdom to me.

But we don't always do that, do we? Often, we let the cares and busyness of life crowd out the joy of God's wonderful gift.

When that happens, even our time with family and friends—or time that could be spent in joyful productivity and fruitfulness—is marred. Overlooking the good in our lives, we find ourselves focusing on the troubles and evils around us, and we end up wishing away our precious time.

I've already used up a considerable number of mornings, so I'm more than ready to start enjoying them on purpose—to be more "in the moments" of my days, to resist wishing them away for any reason, because God is in them with me.

I've decided to enjoy the sunshine and maybe even the rain. I'll smell the coffee and enjoy a cup once in a while—maybe even two or three, if the morning is slow. And I'll be thankful for the day, even if it calls for ironing, as this one does.

Today, enjoy the gift—and don't miss all the other gifts hidden in the package.

"Teach us to number our days,
that we may apply our hearts to wisdom" (Psalm 90:12).

Beginning Again

"Depart from me for I am a sinful man!" Peter's cry rang across the water.

A short time earlier, he'd listened to the teacher with as much respect as anyone else—or so he thought. He'd even been happy to help Jesus by letting him use his boat as a platform. And just a few minutes ago, after Jesus' talk was finished, Peter had done what Jesus told him to do. He went out on the lake to fish one more time even though he'd been certain it would be a waste of time and effort.

Now, at this moment of self-revelation, Peter felt he deserved the smelly slaps on his face as he knelt among the fish, too ashamed to look Jesus in the eye.

What shamed him was the broken net. Jesus had told him to let out his *nets* but he had let out only one—and not his best one at that, because he knew there were no fish to be caught that day. After all, he'd already spent the whole night fishing with nothing to show for it.

That broken net told Jesus (as well as everyone else) that Peter's trust—and, therefore, his obedience—had been half-hearted.

I think I know how Peter felt. There have been times I've looked too long at my own realities (my own world of impossibilities), and my trust in God has weakened. Whenever that happens, my own weakened trust results in the same self-protecting, half-hearted obedience as did Peter's. Before long, I am like Peter—filled with joy-stealing shame.

But comfort comes from Jesus' words to Peter, "Don't be afraid! From now on you'll catch men!"

A fresh start! That's what Jesus offered Peter that day, and that's what he offers all of us: A new beginning—expectant, hopeful, without shame.

Today, start out fresh.

> *"The Lord's mercies . . . are new every morning"*
> (Lamentations 3:22-23).

Times and Seasons

My husband teaches in a business school. One of the concepts I occasionally hear him discuss is an "escalating commitment to a failing course of action"—in other words, *not* knowing when to change direction. Apparently, it is occasionally appropriate to let something go and just be thankful to learn from the experience. To someone like me (persistence is high on my Respected Attribute List) that smacks of giving up or giving in, and I hate both. I have, however, come to see the wisdom in what he teaches.

A while ago, a road I went down didn't take me where I expected to go. I was frustrated, because wasting time bothers me as much as giving up. The failure bothered me because I'd had peace about taking that road, and now I questioned whether someone as dull of hearing as I obviously must be could ever be led by God.

Then I heard Evangelist Jesse Duplantis say, "Your direction is not always your destiny." That took a while to sink in. Eventually, reflecting on my recent disappointment, I realized I might have taken that road for a different reason than I'd first thought. Maybe it was so I'd learn to take risks. Or maybe it was to help me develop skills, knowledge, and relationships that would help me move forward. It could have been for any or all of those reasons. I found all of them on that road.

I now think of changes in direction—even those brought about by negative circumstances—as exciting adventures. New seasons bring new challenges, but new challenges bring new growth, and growth brings new joy. With this newfound perspective, I am free to be led by the Spirit, not by sunk cost, whether that cost is time or money.

May we all know the times and the seasons in our lives—the time to go in and the time to go out—and enter each season with trust and faith in the one who leads.

Today, be open to new things. And be excited!

"Thou shalt guide me with thy counsel and
afterward receive me to glory" (Psalm 73:24).

Just Imagine

I'm delighted beyond words. I am soon to become a grandmother.

It still seems incredible, too wonderful to get my mind around. Maybe none of us can fathom it at first. I've heard many a newly-minted grandmother say, "I can't believe it!"

I don't think our amazement has anything to do with the fact that our children have children, although I'm told that's part of it. I think it has more to do with the fact that we don't feel old enough to be grandparents—not nearly as old as our grandparents seemed to be, or our own parents when we made them grandparents.

Somehow, in spite of having to deal with our bodies' undeniable evidence of the passing years, our minds keep us young.

There are still so many things in this world that feel new to us. New looks, new ideas, new experiences, new places to see, new people to meet. And every twenty-four hours, a brand new day.

I know the writer of Ecclesiastes said there is nothing new under the sun, but—dare I say it?—I think he was wrong, at least in one respect.

Every day *is* new, filled with new mercies and fresh grace, with new challenges and new hope, with new manifestations of God's blessing.

We see it in the face of each new baby.

Today, imagine amazing new things!

> *"But though our outward man perisheth,*
> *our inward man is renewed day by day"* (2 Corinthians 4:16).

To Dream the Impossible Dream

I just put down *Turn Your Dreams into Realities,* by Sue Augustine. It's probably the most practical, biblically accurate and *motivating* motivational book I've read in a while—and very well written to boot.

With short chapters, it's perfect for bedtime reading and with the added benefit of ending the day with positive, hope-filled thoughts. While it's definitely a must read for someone just starting out in life, I expect Augustine's book would help any of us revive some dreams we thought had died.

Dreams are like heart vitamins. Without them we weaken and, eventually, settle into inactivity and fruitlessness. God knows that. That's why he gives them to us—dreams designed especially for who he created us to be, designed so we can share his joy of fruitfulness.

As we read his Word with the express purpose of finding his will, his ways and his voice, we'll begin to sense his very personal dream for us—not all at once, probably, but step by step.

I was going to say "Happy dreaming!" but that's not really the goal. The dream is just the beginning. But, like every beginning, without it nothing happens.

Today, look at who your Father is and remember you were born to greatness.

Let yourself hope again.

Let yourself dream.

"Where there is no vision, the people perish"
(Proverbs 29:18).

Perchance to Dream

Dreams can be elusive things.

This is true, not just in regard to *realizing* them, but also in *recognizing* them.

When I was a teenager, I dreamed of being a writer. But it seemed an impractical, if not impossible, dream. I discarded even the very idea of writing professionally and, instead, became an elementary school teacher.

I can't say it was a mistake; I loved teaching. In fact, back then if anyone had asked if I wanted to write I would have laughed. But years later, I discovered that the dream was still alive. Now I'm working on the novel that was the dream in the first place. I don't know if I'll finish it, but that doesn't matter. I'm enjoying working on it.

I read a great article in the July 2008 edition of *Reader's Digest* by Keith Ferrazzi, the CEO of Ferazzi Greenlight and author of *Never eat Alone*. Here are a few tidbits from the article entitled, "Got a Dream? Here's how to make it happen":

- "Each of us contains seeds of greatness which can be expressed in myriad ways . . ."
- "Don't make the mistake of never committing to anything."
- "Help others help you . . . [You saw that movie, right? Tom Cruise, Cuba Gooding? Listen to trusted critics.]"

If you already have a dream, it may be God given, one that is meant to give you a vision of where he wants to take you. If you have no dream, ask God for one. Ask him to show you his dream for you.

Today, talk to God about dreams.

*"Trust in the Lord and do good; Dwell in the land and feed on his faithfulness. Delight yourself also in the Lord, and he shall give you the desires of your heart. **Commit your way to the Lord; trust also in Him**. And He shall bring it to pass"* (Psalm 37:3-5).

Sure Steps

A number of years ago at our church's New Year's Eve banquet, I was asked to read a poem.

It was about walking into the darkness.

Perhaps an appropriate sentiment for the beginning of a new year—put your hand in God's hand and trust in him.

But it bothered me to refer to walking into the future as walking into the unknown—into darkness. It just didn't seem right. Aren't we supposed to be walking in the light?

I realize that often the future *feels* like a dark, foreboding place, especially bombarded as we are by the news from CNN, NBC, CBC, FOX, et al. The message of that old poem was actually a good one. Trusting God is the key to peace in situations like those we see portrayed on television every day—and in those we live.

But trusting God will result in believing his words—won't it?

Psalm 119 says much about the place of God's Word in our lives. According to the psalmist, it is the ever-present, undimming lamp to our feet and light for our path, no matter how dark the place and times in which we live.

Today, stay close to the light and walk confidently.

"In him is no darkness at all" (1 John 1:5).

ON BELIEVING WORDS

Words are powerful—but only if we believe them.

Words

I just returned home from The Word Guild's *Write! Canada* conference held in Guelph, Ontario. It was a roller-coaster again this year; highs of being with writers and feeling like I might be one of them; lows of recognizing the difficulty of publishing in today's environment.

But every year—and perhaps even more so this year, having listened to beautiful readings of his own work by renowned, award-winning Canadian author Rudy Wiebe—I come away with a renewed respect for the power of words.

There is something awe-inspiring in words "written on pages and held in hands and seen and spoken and thought over and over again," as Mr. Wiebe read, his voice tight with emotion.

Think of it! By *words* we are drawn to our heavenly Father, and by *words* we are born again into His family. "With the mouth confession is made unto salvation."

It is by *words* that we receive encouragement and learn his ways. We even "partake of his divine nature" by his words.

Eloquent or simple, words are precious and powerful.

Today, for just a while, think about something Jesus said.

> *"For I have given them the words which thou gavest me,
> and they have received them"* (John 17:8).

Seeds

Those of us who live in cities might lose sight of this fact, but everything comes from a seed. Trees come from seed. Flowers come from seed. Potatoes, carrots, lettuce and tomatoes all come from seed.

We come from seed.

Most of us remember that Jesus said God's Word is seed.

Every promise of God—from forgiveness to eternal life and everything else that pertains to life and godliness—is given to us in seed form.

We all know that physical seeds have to be planted before they can grow and develop into what they were designed to become. In the same way, it is only when God's Word-seed is planted that it can grow into the harvest it was meant to bring.

Word-seed of any kind has to be planted in the good ground of a steadfast, believing heart.

I wonder how often we plant only a few of the seeds he has provided, and then, when the fruit of the others don't show up, we think God has held out on us.

Today, can you let your heart believe every word?

"The sower soweth the word . . . and they which are sown on good ground; such as hear the word and receive it and bring forth fruit, some thirty fold, some sixty, and some a hundred" (Mark 4:14-20).

Nothing Comes from Nothing

"Somewhere in my youth or childhood, I must have done something good," sang Maria in the classic movie, *The Sound of Music*.

Something always comes from something. Everything starts with a seed. There is no fruit without a seed.

All of the following areas of fruitfulness are mentioned in the Bible:

- "Fruit of the lips"
- "Fruit of thy works"
- "Fruit of hands"
- "Fruit of thoughts"
- "Fruit of doings"
- "Fruit of righteousness"
- "Fruit of the Spirit"
- "Fruit of the Word sown"

Jesus said, after a lengthy discourse on fruitfulness: "If ye abide in me and my words abide in you, you shall ask what ye will and it shall be done unto you. Herein is my Father glorified, that ye bear much fruit; so shall ye be my disciples" (John 15:7, 8).

Here Jesus connects the fruit that glorifies God to the Word-seeds that abide.

We can't make fruit appear and grow, but we can abide. Just as the branch produces fruit by remaining attached to the tree, we produce the fruit God plans for us by abiding in him and letting the word abide in us. And just as that tree and branch have activity going on—sap and nutrients flowing—that we can't see, we can have activity going on that people around us might not see.

Today, it's not too late to do some farming!

"While the earth remains, seed time and harvest,
cold and heat, winter and summer,
and day and night shall not cease" (Genesis 8:22).

Is it, or isn't it?

My self-talk always includes encouragement to trust what God's Word says about a subject, more than I trust what I see around me. That might sound strange and unreasonable to some who might hear me, so that's why I rarely self-talk out loud!

Some might wonder how I can believe *what I can't see* more than *what I can see*. Or how I can believe that *what I can't see yet*, really and truly *is*!

Understandably, the uninitiated might say we can *hope* for what isn't (yet), but to believe *it is so* in the face of evidence to the contrary is foolish at best, presumptuous at worst.

But if we could go back a few years and follow Jesus around, we would hear him doing it all the time. He believed what wasn't, in spite of what was.

He said, "Woman, thou art loosed," when she wasn't yet.

He said, "Go show yourself to the priest," to lepers who should only go if they were pure, when they weren't yet.

He said to Jairus, who had just been told his daughter had died, "Fear not, and she shall be made whole," and to the mourners, "She sleepeth!" when she was dead.

Is it possible Jesus wanted them to believe what he said, even though it was the opposite of what they could see?

Today, choose to believe first.

"Jesus saith unto her, Said I not unto thee, that, if thou wouldest believe, thou shouldest see the glory of God" (John 11:39-41).

Casey Comes Home

Casey is our cat. A grey, black and white tabby, Casey started life in a barn near Lobo, Ontario. The barn was full of cats and kittens, so we don't know if it was his mother we saw kicking him away when he tried to feed. For whatever reason, Casey wasn't getting much to eat and was in quite a state when we met him. Skinny and weak, he was a pitiful sight.

"I don't think that little guy is going to make it," my friend who owns the farm said in a tone most pitying.

Actually, she didn't have to say a word. He had us at one look. The scrawny, weak, sad little one came home with us and became part of the Rowe household.

We called him Kitty Cat first because we weren't sure of his gender. That eventually abbreviated to K.C., and finally, after we got to know him better, Casey. Now he's often just The Case because he defines the term.

He loved to be held and cuddled when he first arrived, but he didn't have a clue how to eat or drink. I dropper-fed and watered him for a week until he got the hang of it. Today, he has more than adequately made up for lost time, and demands food on a regular schedule—his own schedule. He not only defied the odds, he's thriving.

It really did take Casey a while to get into the swing of things, but think about it: Sometimes it even takes *us* a while to find out who we really are, what we can do, and where we belong.

Today, look in God's Word and see who you are.

*"Now therefore ye are (through Him) no more strangers
and foreigners, but fellow citizens with the saints, and of the household of
God"* (Ephesians 2:19).

Parched

It rained that Saturday, all day.

I'm sure it had nothing to do with the fact that my husband and I had just pruned back to almost nothing the bush that blocked the sprinkler head. And nothing to do with the new sprinkler I had bought to give the grass a longer watering than the automated sprinkler was willing to do.

Poor lawn! It's terrible what lack of water will do to a patch of grass.

Our poor parched patch had been deprived of water for at least two summers so you can imagine how it looked. (Yes, we should have figured out the problem much earlier!) Varieties of weeds I had never before encountered had moved in. The few tenacious blades of grass that had managed to survive in hard dirt were crying out for help—for life sustaining water.

Our bodies do that, too. If we don't drink, we become tired and listless. Our muscles ache or begin to cramp. Dehydration is not pretty and, worse, is dangerous—especially if it takes us a while to identify the problem.

Our souls and spirits need water too, the kind that can only be found in one place. Its lack, however, is not always obvious. Sometimes, everything around us looks good and we are happy with the circumstances of the moment, but if we get quiet we can tell that something is not right. Something is missing. Some life-giving spring—maybe the one that brings peace that stays, hope that has reason, and joy that strengthens—has dried up.

At times like that, all we need is the soul refreshment that comes from looking at Jesus' face, and the spirit life that comes from the water of his word.

Today, let's check our water supply.

"Oh God, thou art my God; early will I seek thee:
my soul thirsteth for thee, my flesh longest for thee in a dry and thirsty land,
where no water is" (Psalm 63:1).

911

One morning, amidst the official remembrances of those who perished in the Twin Towers of the World Trade Center on September 11, 2001, there was a story of a different kind—the story of twin girls born that day in New York City. The parents talked about the joy they felt, undimmed by the horror of the day.

The report should have been warm and comforting, but it wasn't. Not for me. For me it was disturbing.

What bothered me about this story wasn't the reporter's statement that when these little girls were grown enough to know what their birth date meant to the nation, they thought they had been responsible for the many deaths that occurred that day. After all, it isn't strange for children to feel as if they are the center of the universe and, therefore, think they have much more effect on that world than they actually do. And these girls eventually came to know they had nothing to do with the tragedy.

What most disturbed me was the mother's take on the juxtaposition of joy and sorrow. According to the anchor reporting the story, the mother felt that *in order for someone to be born into the world, someone had to leave!*

I found it difficult to believe she meant it. Surely, I hoped, she couldn't be so ignorant of spiritual realities! But maybe she did, and maybe she was. And that made me sad. Can it be that the prophet Hosea pegs the problem when he says, "There is no truth, mercy, or knowledge of God in the land" (Hosea 4:1)? And again when he reports God's words, "My people are destroyed for lack of knowledge" (Hosea 4:6).

Lack of knowledge is debilitating in any situation, but lack of knowledge of God weakens us all and destroys many.

Today, love the truth.

"For the Lord gives wisdom: out of his mouth cometh knowledge and understanding" (Proverbs 2:6).

Paul and Festus

Paul was in trouble again. His Jewish brothers were in an uproar over his teaching, accusing him of inciting the people. A Roman commander—hoping to settle them down—had soldiers remove Paul from the mob and hold him in barracks overnight. Later that evening, Paul's nephew caught wind of a plan devised by forty Jews in which they were to lay in wait and kill Paul the next day as he was being transferred to the venue where he was to face his accusers. He immediately got word to the commander who forestalled more trouble by sending Paul to Governor Felix in Caesarea.

Governor Felix kept him in prison for two years, during which time Paul and Felix visited often—Paul reasoning with him about righteousness, self-control and the judgment to come.

After two years, Festus replaced Felix as governor. King Agrippa came to town to greet the new governor and eventually Paul found himself in a discussion with them both. Having heard the trumped up accusations against Paul, King Agrippa gave him the opportunity to speak for himself.

Paul went into a long treatise about his background, his meeting with Jesus on the road to Damascus, and all that followed. When he got to his belief that Jesus was the Christ who would be the first to rise from the dead and would proclaim light to the Gentiles—Gentiles like Festus and Agrippa—Festus couldn't take it anymore.

"Paul, you are . . . mad!" he said with a loud voice.

"I am not mad, most noble Festus, but speak words of truth and reason," was the reply.

How I love Paul's answer! He wasn't apologetic; he didn't try to soften the effect; and he didn't pretend that faith is unreasonable.

Today, know your faith is based on words of truth and reason.

> *"But sanctify the Lord God in your hearts: and be ready always to give an answer to every man that asketh you a **reason** of the hope that is in you with meekness and fear"* (1 Peter 3:14-16).

Paul at Sea

A series of challenges by his Jewish brothers brought Paul first before Felix and then before Festus and King Agrippa, before he finally appealed to Caesar as a Roman citizen. After that, at the time of this story, Paul was among other prisoners in the custody of a centurion named Julius, sailing to Italy on their way to Rome.

During a stopover in Fair Haven, near Lasea, Paul, not one to keep his opinions to himself, told his custodian and the captain that they should winter there because of the time of the year—the fast was already over and sailing was about to become dangerous.

They didn't listen to Paul, and immediately set sail. A storm came up and before long they were in "all manner" of trouble. For many days they saw no sun or moon because of the storm clouds and pelting rain and driving winds. Finally, after throwing as much as they could overboard in an attempt to avoid grounding, they gave up hope.

Paul stepped up and told them not to worry; he'd heard from God. God had promised to protect his life and the lives of all the men if they would listen to him. He said that if they would stay on the ship until they ran aground—and they *would* run aground—they would all survive.

Some believed, but others didn't. When the unbelievers started to leave the ship in a small skiff, Paul told the others, "Unless these stay, you cannot be saved." Imagine the tension of the moment as the soldiers cut the skiff loose to keep everyone on board!

In spite of the drama, Paul held firm. He told them, "I believe God that it will be just as it was told me." And it was.

Has God told us anything?

Today, even if the storm rages, let's believe it will be just as he has said.

"And so it was that they all escaped safely to land" (Acts 27:44).

Saving Faith?

One lazy day I was reading Hebrews, a book I like to read at one sitting because I can misread it if I miss the context. As I read chapter eleven, the famous "Hall of Faith" chapter, I flashed back to a time when I really didn't know what faith was.

I knew I *had* faith because I believed in God and trusted in Jesus for my salvation. I knew that whatever faith was, it was also the substance of things hoped for and the evidence of things not seen. But that didn't help me identify it. "Substance and evidence" seemed like synonyms, not a definition.

When finally I realized that I was saved by grace *through faith*, and that I was saved *by believing* something (with the heart man believes unto righteousness), and confessing its truth (with the mouth confession is made unto salvation) that finally helped me sort it out. Faith, obviously, was connected to believing in some way—believing something specific.

Saving faith came from believing that Jesus died for *my* sins and then acting on that by accepting him as *my* Savior and Lord. The salvation was offered universally, but enacted individually by personal belief and the act of personally receiving by—well—saying so.

In almost every century, there arises the teaching that, because of God's grace, everyone will eventually receive salvation. But the proponents of this error have forgotten that man was made in God's image and therefore has the ability and responsibility to make his own choice. They forget that man's salvation has two activators: grace and faith. It is by grace; it is through faith. Through believing something by choice and acting on it on purpose.

Today, live by faith on purpose.

"Believe on the Lord Jesus Christ and thou shalt be saved"
(Acts16:31).

Famous Believers' Hall of Faith

Everyone listed in Hebrews 11 believed something that moved them to act—something that could be expressed in words. Even though we aren't told exactly what some of them believed, we can surmise what it was.

Obviously, Noah believed and acted when God told him the flood was coming and whoever would get into that famous—infamous, at the time—ark would be saved.

Abraham believed and acted when God said there was a promised land out there somewhere for him, and again (later) when he said that Abraham's promised seed would spring from Isaac. In these cases we're told that "by faith" Abraham sojourned in a strange land, and "by faith" he proceeded to offer Isaac as an offering, which—as far as God was concerned—he did figuratively.

Sarah, after a slow start, believed the angel's message that she would have a child, and did.

Abel gave his excellent offering *by faith.* It's not clear exactly what he believed, but according to Verse 6, the very least we must all believe is that God "is" and that he rewards those who seek him. So I wonder if Abel gave the offering *believing that God would receive it and reward him for it,* and *that* was the faith that pleased God. Even though we might assume his offering of the animal pleased God more than his brother's grain offering—perhaps because of the eventual blood sacrifice—nothing says that, outright. And since the focus of this chapter is faith, there had to be something of faith which pleased God in the offering.

These all received their specific promises in their lifetime. What they didn't receive was the greater promise of Jesus coming, but they died "in faith" still believing in that heavenly city they looked for.

Today, what here-and-now promise will you believe and act on?

"So then, faith comes by hearing, and hearing by the word of God"
(Romans 10:17).

Blessed Are They

It was Thanksgiving Day. We gave thanks for life's bounty and celebrated with a gorgeous 26 lb. turkey—the stuffing made, of course, with Mount Scio savoury from Newfoundland—and pumpkin pie baked at a genius bakery at The Beaches in Toronto.

Surrounded by a mix of family, friends, and acquaintances of family or friends, we were very thankful.

It's easy—and right—to be grateful for and rejoice in what we see.

But we can also be thankful for the things we can't see: love, faith, hope, and promises.

After Jesus was raised from the dead, he was visiting with his disciples for the second time. Thomas was there this time. He had missed Jesus' last visit, and he didn't quite buy Mary Magdalene's and the other disciples' stories about having seen him. Even now, he didn't give that "My Lord and My God," response until after Jesus invited him to touch his scars.

I wonder if he reached out and touched Jesus *before* he believed.

I often have to remind myself of Jesus' comment to Thomas, "Blessed are they that have not seen, and yet have believed."

I remind myself that those who have not yet seen the promises fulfilled, but still believe and are thankful, are blessed.

Be blessed today!

"Be careful for nothing, but in everything, by prayer and supplication with thanksgiving, let your requests be made known to God" (Philippians 4:6).

24

Ye Shall Know the Truth

My pastor read from a translation which quotes Jesus in this way: "The Father is seeking those who will worship him in spirit and in truth (reality)" (John 4:23). "Reality" was the addition of the translators—perhaps innocent, or maybe an example of biblical revisionism.

I used to wonder how one could possibly worship God in spirit but not in truth. I thought maybe it was just saying the same thing in two ways—that God doesn't want fake praise (hypocrisy in worship), which is what the word "reality" seems to imply.

But earlier in Jesus' chat with the woman, he clarifies what comes next when he says, "You worship you *know not* what; we *know* what we worship." He's talking about knowing what or whom you worship.

He goes on to say that God is seeking worshipers who worship in spirit and in truth. When we connect that to what he said earlier, we see he was referring to God's desire that we worship with *accurate knowledge of him*.

The word translated "truth" here is the one translated "truth" in John 8:32. "Ye shall know the truth and the truth shall set you free." Not truth, or honesty, in us. *Truth about God*!

But does it matter if we get that wrong? What's the big deal?

If we believe God's Word is bread to us—a life-giving necessity rather than something we only pay attention to on Sundays or when we're in trouble—then any alteration of the composition of that bread should be of concern to us. Biblical revisionism, changing the thought of a statement, is concerning.

Truth about God, and therefore truth in our own worship, is something we should be unwilling to do without. If God is unwilling that we should be without it, should we settle for less?

Today, let's decide not to settle.

"Behold, thou desirest truth in the inward parts:
and in the hidden part thou shalt make me to know wisdom"
(Psalm 51:5-7).

25

Like a Child

Mike Shreve, in his book *God's Promises for your Children*, says: "Real praise is not practiced, polished, professional, or performed. It is simple, sincere, humble, heartfelt, spontaneous and full of passion toward the Most High." He continues, "Jesus claimed [Matt 21:16] that God perfects this kind of praise in children."

In an article in the June 6, 2008 edition of *Christian Week Magazine*, Stephanie Douglas quoted American theologian and worship leader Marva Dawn. This caught my attention: "I don't think we should ever study worship without theology, because un-theological worship is not true worship . . . Styles don't matter . . . You need to know the God you're worshiping."

I recall a particular day when my worship might well have been at its highest, even though without eloquence or beauty of presentation. I was sitting at my kitchen table, drinking coffee, reading my Bible and learning some things about my Father that I had never known before. I paused, took a deep breath and said, "Wow."

If we find ourselves mechanically speaking or singing praise and worship, all it takes is a long look at our Father—seeing in the Bible who he is and what he has done through his Son—to bring some real, honest, heartfelt praise.

Today, read what he says and choose to believe it. And praise him for it.

"And he said, Lord, I believe. And he worshiped him"
(John 9:37-39).

The Living Word

At church that morning we sang a song that had this line in it:

"Your word is living in my heart."

As I sang, I thought about how it's possible for me to have all kinds of knowledge of the word, but still not have it *living* in my heart. If I'm not careful, it can remain dormant and unfruitful.

I thought about the children of Israel who died in the wilderness. The book of Hebrews says it was because of their unbelief that they didn't enter into their promised land. It says that "the word they heard had no effect, not being mixed with faith in those who heard it" (Hebrews 4:2).

The same thing happened when Jesus visited his own home town. He could do no great works there "because of their unbelief." The word had no effect on them or in them, even coming from him. I guess they wouldn't believe it when he said he was anointed to set them free. They had all heard the word, but in them it had no life—no fruit that it was meant to produce.

Any word from God, written in the book or spoken in our heart, can lie dormant until we decide to believe it and act on it, on purpose.

If you have any doubt that *believing* is a choice, look at the elections we are blessed to take part in every few years. What a challenge to decide whom to believe and which words to act upon! We don't know the people. We can't see into the future to see if their ideas will work, or even if they'll do what they say they'll do. We can look back on their past actions and hopefully make some educated guesses, but that's all. In spite of the challenge, however, many of us will do just that: make a decision whom to believe.

Today, choose to believe God and see what happens.

> *"Now may the God of hope fill you with joy*
> *and peace in believing* [the word], *that you may abound in hope by the*
> *power of the Holy Ghost"* (Romans 15:13).

Believing Like Jesus

Jesus was having a few interesting days in Jerusalem. He had just annoyed the well-respected Pharisees by healing a sick man he found lying near the pool called Bethesda near the Sheep Gate. The healing itself might have gotten a pass, but it was the Sabbath and that created a problem. Then, adding even more offence to healing on that day, Jesus told the man to pick up his bed and walk! On the Sabbath! When challenged about it, Jesus told them, "My Father has been working until now, and I have been working."

To tell you the truth, I don't know what he meant by that—although he talked later about only doing what he saw his father doing, connecting his works to God's—but the fact that he called God *his father* was the last straw for them. *He was making himself equal with God!* They tried to kill him for it.

So Jesus went into a long (page and a half) discourse about the Father and the Son and their relationship, and then gave two witnesses to the fact that he is really the son—John said it, and the works said it.

But then Jesus confesses *he* needs no evidence of who he is other than that of one, his Father: *"There is another who bears witness of me and **I know that the witness which He witnesses of me is true** . . . You search the scriptures because you believe that in them you have eternal life; and **these are they which testify of me.** But you are not willing to come to me that you might have life"* (John 5:32-40).

Jesus knew that what God said about him in scripture was true. He needed no other witness. Do we believe what God has said about him—and about us—in scripture? Or do we look for another witness?

Today, let's think about who has given "witness" to our salvation, every part of it, and believe.

"Jesus said to him, 'Go your way, your son lives.' So the man believed the word Jesus spoke to him and he went his way" (John 4:50).

Everyone a Winner

God is able to make everyone a winner!

Is it hard to grasp the concept that he would want to—even if you can believe it's possible?

Just think about a parent's attitude toward his or her children. I have only one child, so those who have multiple blessings of the two-legged sort will probably understand it even better than I.

There's no desire—is there?—for any one of our children to outstrip the others, or for one who is excelling to be brought low to make the others feel better.

The parent's heart is the same for all. They want that they all live excellent, happy, and productive lives; that each new day will bring an outshining of the day before; that they are all front runners in life's race, leaving opponents such as depression, sadness, lack, sickness, and inferiority in their dust.

Think about this: Surely, one who has the wisdom and knowledge to create worlds can create several billions of winners.

Feel good gospel? No, just good news!

Today, believe some good news.

*"God is able to make all grace abound toward you
so that you always having all sufficiency of all things, may abound unto
every good work"* (2Corinthians 9:8).

Earthshaking

That morning, over a steaming cup of Tetley, I read in Psalm 91, "His truth **shall be** your **shield** and **buckler**" and "You shall not be afraid of the terror by night."

The words "shield and buckler" jumped off the page. It occurred to me—not for the first time, I'm sure, but perhaps more dramatically given what had happened earlier—that people are protected behind shields. Bucklers, too, are tools of protection, more of an "all sides" thing like a soldier's armor.

But what struck me at that reading was the fact that shields and bucklers have no effect if we don't do something with them. We have to hide behind them, or in them. They don't help us if they're just sitting there, even though they are powerful. Left on the floor, or in a closet or on a night table, they do nothing.

God's truth, his word, *is* powerful but it *"shall be"* effective in our lives when we interact with it and believe it and put our weight on it. We put it between ourselves and our enemies when we put it in our own mouths, and when we rest on it as on a solid rock.

There had been an earthquake in Los Angeles earlier that day. My daughter felt it as she prepared to photograph headshots of a celebrity at the Hotel Bel-Ayr in Los Angeles. She knows who and what her shield is, and told me later that she wasn't afraid when the earth shook.

That did her mother's heart good!

Today, live on the rock and hide behind God's Word.

"His truth shall be thy shield and buckler" (Psalm 91:4).

ON NEVER GIVING UP

Hope springs eternal.

Don't shut up the spring.

Out of the Mouths of Babes

One Sunday there was a huge wheelhouse built on the platform in the sanctuary because the church was running an evening program for church and neighborhood kids. The theme of the week-long event had to do with ships and pirates.

Sometime during the week, the "captain"—holding a long spyglass for effect—had talked to the children about God sightings. Referring to different things they had seen God do during the course of their adventure at sea, the captain then asked the children, "Why are God sightings important?"

A little girl raised her hand and said, "Because they give us hope."

Out of the mouths of babes!

May our own God sightings give us hope for the journey!

May we never become so hardened in our hearts that we find no hope in someone else's God sighting.

May we always be watchful to see who needs the hope our God sightings will bring.

Today, look for God.

"We will not hide them from their children, shewing to the generation to come the praises of the Lord, and his strength, and his wonderful works that he hath done [God sightings]. *For he established a testimony in Jacob, and appointed a law in Israel, which he commanded our fathers, that they should make them known to their children: That the generation to come might know them, even the children which should be born . . . that they might set their hope in God"* (Psalm 78:3-6).

Our Greatest Gift

One Saturday I attended a homeschooling conference. One of my friends, a novelist and author of a book on homeschooling, was a speaker at the event. She had suggested that my book *Keepers of the Testimony* would be a good fit for the book table she was setting up since it speaks to sharing our faith with our children.

We had a very busy day, handing out postcards and bookmarks and chatting with other vendors and the hundreds of parents wandering through the huge facility from 8:00 A.M. until 5:00 P.M. As I handed a *Keepers* bookmark to one gentleman, I quoted the back cover introduction, "The best gift we can give our children."

He quickly retorted, "That would be love and attention!"

Just as quickly I replied, "Well, yes, that would be true," a little embarrassed that I had overlooked something so obvious.

As I thought more about it, however, I decided he was wrong, and I was wrong to agree. (Not that I should have disagreed at that moment!)

Of course, the first and last thing we should give our children *is* love and attention. It's like life-breath to a child; it should be a constant. But many children, well-loved and attended, have lived and died without knowledge of the goodness of God. And that is sad, no matter what other precious gifts they were given.

It's sad because the testimony of God's goodness is an inheritance that will empower not just for a lifetime, but forever. It is hope that never ends.

Today, I will stand my ground on that one.

"Thy testimonies have I taken as a heritage forever: for they are the rejoicing of my heart" (Psalm 119:111).

Blue Monday

It was long past my regular bedtime when I finally admitted the color of the day. It had been a Blue Monday, I decided, and I figured I might as well go to bed and put an end to it.

I'm not sure what caused it, but I blamed it on having spent the whole morning at the car dealership waiting for them to put the new winter tires on my car—tires I had just bought at the exorbitant cost of $1350.00. Maybe the price wasn't all that bad, but since I hate snow—except for its initial pristine arrival—the thought of it costing me money is upsetting any day.

Then I had to take my old winter coat to the tailor to be hemmed and retooled because I couldn't find a new one I liked.

And I still couldn't decide on the publisher's fresh offerings of a cover for the new book.

As I put on my pyjamas and climbed into bed, I looked back over my complaints and saw the light. I reviewed my day and my complaints and decided they were all, by and large, quite lovely. Certainly, none of them qualified as "how are they increased that trouble me; . . . many there be which say of my soul 'there is no help for her in God.'" as David moaned in Psalm 3.

But then, even though my Blue Monday had very little reason for its funk, my comfort should never be found in the meagreness of my troubles.

After all, *days* can't be counted on to bring me joy. But the Lord can—every day.

Let him lift your head today.

"Thou, O Lord, art a shield for me;
my glory and the lifter up of mine head" (Psalm 3:3).

Let the Weak Say Something

I read Psalm 18 just about every day. It starts off with, "I will love you, O Lord, my strength."

That, right there, is one of the most powerful things I have ever learned. Someone else is my strength.

Think of it this way: When a child is born, the strength of his life is his parents. A little baby has no ability to care for itself. No wisdom, no understanding, no knowledge base—nothing, in fact, but life and breath and potential.

We, too, have life, breath and potential. We also have experience, education, contacts, physical strength, talents—the list could go on. But still, even at our very best, without God we are weak. The dark valley called earth has too many dangers we can't handle on our own.

But have you noticed we hate to need outside help?

In our society, we don't like weakness, either in ourselves or in others. That aversion suggests to me that we creatures, made in God's image, were never intended to be weak. But we are; it's obvious. Without God, we have no real strength in the battleground that is earth.

But we are not without God, or don't have to be.

That's why I love Psalm 18 and why I make no apologies for my hope that "It is God that arms me with strength, and makes my way perfect. He makes my feet like the feet of deer, and sets me on my high places" (Psalm 18:32, 33).

Today let the weak say, "I am strong."

"My God shall be my strength" (Isaiah 49:5).

The Building

On my daily walk I take a route that passes by a building site. When I started walking this route a couple of years back, the lot was vacant and pretty much overtaken with weeds and decaying matter like fallen branches and such.

But for many months now I've watched as a transformation took place, from empty lot to empty lot with huge hole, to messy lot full of a tangle of metal.

Every day I looked in vain to find out what that mess was to become, hoping something pleasant would overlook the brook where I saw Bambi (another story, another day). As the structure began to take shape, I could see that the designers had put considerable thought into its functionality and beauty, as well as its ability to take advantage of the beauty around it. But still, I could find no clue as to what its end might be.

Then one day I saw the sign: Coming Soon, Luxury Retirement Living.

I finally knew what the builder had in mind.

1 Corinthians 3:9 says, "Ye are God's building." God is at work, building something wonderful. But he's not building alone. We're building right alongside him. Psalm 32:8 says that God will instruct us and teach us in the way we should go; and, in Matthew's account of the gospel story, Jesus tells us that if we hear (and, obviously, believe) and do Jesus' sayings, then we build wisely.

That encourages me, because no matter what is going on in my life, if I let God get involved—and remain patient, trusting his heart, believing his words and obeying his voice—the matter will have a good end.

And I will see it.

Today, think about what God is building in your life, and listen for his voice.

"Behold the upright: for the end of that man is peace."
(Psalm 37:37).

Lunch with Jesus

This story is in John's gospel, and the similarity between this scene and the first time we saw interaction between Jesus and Peter is remarkable. In the first meeting, remember, Peter had fished all night and caught nothing. Jesus told him to let down the nets, but Peter let down only one net which broke with the catch.

Again this time, Peter has fished all night and caught nothing. A stranger on the shore calls out, "Throw the net to the other side of the boat and you'll catch some." Peter does so and the net fills up. 153 big fish, the story says. They take another look at the stranger. John is the first to recognize Jesus and cries out, "It's the Lord!" The risen Lord! Peter, ever the impulsive one, jumps out and swims or wades to shore.

What follows soon after seems like a flashback to Peter's denial of Jesus, but this time Jesus gives him the opportunity to make a new commitment and a new memory. With eyes probing but gentle, Jesus asks, "Peter, do you love me?" Three times, he asks—reflecting Peter's three denials. And three times Peter expresses his love and accepts the call: Feed my sheep.

Later when Jesus prophesied Peter's end, Peter looked over at John and asked Jesus about *his* future. Perhaps Jesus looked at him kindly and smiled before he replied, "Peter, what is that to thee? Follow me." *No matter what is going on in anyone else's life, Peter, follow me. Don't compare yourself to anyone, Peter. Follow me. I've told you how this will end, Peter, and I'll be with you even then. Follow me.* Precious!

Jesus words have etched on my heart this truth: Even though my relationship with God is the same as others'—he is our Father and our God—it is unquestionably, intensely personal. Just as he had a path for Peter different from that of John, he has a path for me. As I look back, I see his presence and provision on that path. He's been with me, just as he was with Peter and the others that day on the banks of the lake—just as he is with you.

Today, remember there's a good path with your name on it.

"But the path of the just is as the shining light, that shineth more and more unto the perfect day" (Proverbs 4:17-19).

Papyrus and Pitch

The guest speaker talked about God's promises. To Abraham God's promise was to make him a father of *many* nations. An impossible promise, because it came when his wife, Sarah, was 89 and he was 99. But a miracle happened. They had Isaac.

Fast forward a few generations. Abraham's seed, now known as Israelites, were slaves in Egypt. They had increased greatly as the promise had said, but their numbers made the new Pharaoh nervous. He devised a brilliant plan to curb the growth of the Hebrew nation—drown the baby boys in the Nile.

That's when the ancient promise became problematic to the seed.

Mark Griffin's story-telling skill helped us imagine a young Levite couple praying, "Please, God, no babies now." After the pregnancy was announced, the prayer might have been, "Please, God, a little girl." After Moses was born, his mom and dad decided to hide him in the bulrushes in a basket made of papyrus and pitch, watched by his sister. Now the prayer must have been, "Please God, keep him quiet."

Watch this moment: The beautiful Egyptian princess, accompanied by her equally beautiful attendants, approaches the Nile in preparation to bathe. Now the prayer becomes, "Please, God, have them go the other way." When the princess and her entourage move in their direction, and then come right to the river bank where Moses is hidden, Miriam prays, "Please, God, keep him *really* quiet, *now!*"

All prayers unanswered because God had a plan, too!

The princess hears the baby's cry and sees Moses. She's smitten right away, even knowing he was a Hebrew. Moses' sister quickly comes out of hiding and, perhaps tentatively, presents an idea, "Let me find a Hebrew woman to care for him."

Now God's plan to uphold his promise to Abraham begins to take shape. Moses, the God-ordained deliverer of God's people, was saved from the enemy's hand by the enemy's own daughter! And his mother got to take care of him, and—I love this—she was *paid* to do it!

Today, no matter what's going on, take hope.

"For he established a testimony in Jacob . . . that they should make them known [God's praises, strength, and works] *. . . that they might set their hope in God"* (Psalm 78:5-7).

Hope Springs Eternal

Who said that? Shakespeare? I'll have to check it out.[1]

Whoever said it knew what he was talking about, at least to a degree. The truth is that hope springs as long as its source remains. When the source runs out, so does the hope.

What got me thinking about hope today was the e-mail I received, supposedly, from the Coca Cola Company, London office. Apparently, they have stashed away, in a bank somewhere, 1,000,000 pounds, British currency, all for me!

How wonderful! How quickly I thought of all the places I could spend the dollars those pounds would translate into! How soon my hope died as I recognized the fragile nature of my source!

The email looked remarkably like last week's similar email from a bank in South Africa that had bags of money just waiting for my check—I forget the amount—which, of course they needed in order to expedite the delivery of my millions. It was reminiscent, too, of the California-based company that promised to advertise my "For Sale by Owner" house, for twice its worth, to Asian investors who apparently didn't care what they bought as long as they had money invested in Canada. All I needed to do was let them charge a mere $675 U.S. to my credit card. Apparently, those fine folks saw my private sale ad in our local paper and, since the ad conveniently told them my departure date, they knew when I would be desperate and, therefore, when they should call.

Talk about hope! I guess the perpetrators of these "opportunities" live in hope, too. Their hope is based, no doubt, on the belief that many of us don't realize that, without a secure foundation, what looks like hope may actually be fantasy.

Today, and always, check out the source.

> "And now, Lord, what wait I for? My hope is in Thee"
> (Psalm 39:7).

---

[1]   Alexander Pope, An Essay on Man, Epistle 1, 1733

Bambi Returns

It started at the beginning of the week with my own prayer time; then it came from a book by C.S. Lewis, then two speakers at our church, and finally a speaker on a television program. By the end of the week four people on as many consecutive days had mentioned a verse in Psalm 18, "He makes my feet like hind's feet and causes me to walk on my high places."

On Friday of that week I was on my daily walk, which I had done for years, and as I crossed the bridge before the empty lot, I looked down at the river and saw a beautiful deer on its banks. We stood and looked at each other for quite a while and then she left, pausing several times to look back before she ran—effortlessly, gracefully—through the nearby wood. I held my breath! "He makes my feet like hind's feet!"

One day much later as I walked by what once was the empty lot, I was thinking I'd probably never see Bambi there again, with all the construction going on and the paved walk by the river now fenced in. I finished the first half of the walk, and then turned around, heading for home. This time, as I crossed the bridge, I was thinking about the Huntley Street interview of the week before, encouraging myself that God is the one who finishes the work. As always, I glanced up river to look for Bambi, just in case.

There she was, leaping over the fence near the river, across the road and the next fence, and off into the woods. My beautiful friend and faithful witness of the truth of Psalm 18! "**He** makes my feet . . ." I gasped when I saw her, and then again as another deer, maybe her offspring, followed her. "**God** is the one . . ."

I know most of you, probably all, have had such natural events point out to you how lovingly God watches over you and encourages you when you need it, so I'm sharing this for those who aren't used to seeing the finger of God in such things.

Today, ask God to open your eyes to see them.

> *"Today, if you will hear his voice* [or see his hand]
> *harden not your heart"* (Psalm 95:7, 8).

Fuel

When I was diagnosed with cancer in 2001, my primary care physician arranged an appointment for me with a surgeon who was purported to be one of the very best in his field. During my meeting with him, I felt my hope drain. It seemed he had already decided I was doomed. As I hurried down the hospital corridor after our meeting, I promised myself I'd never see him again. I'd find another surgeon.

I knew I would not survive without hope—without a vision of life beyond cancer.

From Erwin Raphael McManus' wonderful book *Soul Cravings*:

- Where there is no future there is no hope . . . . And the strange thing about it is that while hope is connected to the future, it is impossible to thrive in the present without it.
- Our ability to endure, to persevere, to overcome is fuelled by this one seemingly innocuous ingredient called hope.
- The goal of spirituality is not to extract from you all desire and passion. The call of Jesus is the exact opposite—delight in him and he will give you the desires of your heart.

These remind me that Jesus said he was come that we might have "life . . . more abundant." Is it possible the word "more" indicates not just comparison, but something related to the continual growth and movement that hope encourages?

Jesus also talked a fair bit about seeking in order to find. We won't do any of the seeking, searching, or knocking without first finding hope. To use one of McManus' favorite words, these all are *fuelled* by hope, and hope is *fuelled* by God.

Today, refuse to live without hope.

"Remember thy word unto thy servant
upon which thou hast caused me to hope" (Psalm 119: 49).

Go for Gold

I was a sports fan for a couple of weeks. From the opening ceremony of the 21st Winter Olympics to the closing celebration, our television was tuned to the games. I cheered at the awards, cried at the poignancy of Joannie Rochette's skate, held my breath when bobsledders crashed out, and felt the pain of those who grieved over missing their goal by a fraction of a second. I also hooted and hollered with joy at that final goal in the men's hockey gold game. It was quite a ride. It brought home to me, once again, how, when all is said and done, we were born to win.

In fact, not only does our heart almost burst at the point of winning, the striving itself brings a special kind of joy. Even failures are worth the effort. (Without the occasional setback, we probably aren't attempting much!)

When we're smart, however, we learn from the failures. The lessons derived from loss are evidence of God's ability and willingness to turn whatever life throws at us to our good—and that is precious. They become well worth the pain of disappointment as they eventually help build our road to success.

Some might say the growth that comes from struggle is the whole point. I tend to mostly disagree with that perspective, although I understand where it comes from.

But I know this without question: We came honestly by the both desire to win and the willingness to persevere—to press for the mark. They are both part of the spiritual DNA of every human being, with good reason and purpose.

Today, let's think like winners.

> "Let us run with patience the race that is set before us, Looking unto Jesus . . . ; who **for the joy that was set before him** endured the cross, despising the shame, and is set down at the right hand of the throne of God. For consider him that endured such contradiction of sinners against himself, lest ye be wearied and faint in your minds" (Hebrews 1-3).

Living in Gerar

A story in the book of Genesis records a time much like the one we're living in. *The Evening News* was depressing. Talking heads were full of gloom and doom and looking for someone to blame. People were very nervous about the future and hoarding whatever they could. The ability to provide the necessities of life was at a back-breaking low. Times were uncertain and prospects for the future were bleak. No one was sowing new crops, for sure. There would be no point; nothing would grow. Many were looking for literal "greener pastures" somewhere else. Some looked to Egypt.

As the story goes, God said to Isaac, "Don't go down to Egypt. Dwell in the land of which I tell you . . . I will be with thee and bless thee." So Isaac listened and stayed in Gerar.

Notice that he had a promise and direction, and he believed and obeyed. Later on we read that not only did he stay in Gerar, he didn't act like everyone else there. Isaac actually *sowed* in famine and, sure enough, the Lord blessed him so much that he became very strong: He "waxed great"—so great that the King became nervous and asked him to leave! Later the king came to him in Beersheba, where he eventually ended up, and asked him to make a covenant of peace since "thou art now the blessed of the Lord."

Interesting stuff! Stranger than fiction!

The theme of my book *Keepers of the Testimony* is that our stories about God's involvement in our lives are supposed to provide hope to the hearers—our children, or anyone else for that matter. The stories are not just meant to be instructive; they are intended to provide vision and hope.

Is there any hope for us in Isaac's story? Is there a *minute* possibility that, even in our economy, if we listen to God's promise and direction, we might just see his blessing—even in famine?

Today, listen and act.

"The Lord knows the days of the upright, And their inheritance shall be forever. They shall not be ashamed in the evil time, And in the days of famine they shall be satisfied" (Psalm 37:18, 19).

Still the Same

God intended for testimonies to carry hope.

We don't always see them that way. We more often see them as carriers of praise, but a huge part of the function and purpose of our stories is to create hope. And the hope is not just for others.

In Psalm 18, we see that on the day of his great deliverance from King Saul, the psalmist David starts off praising God for what he has done—for being his strength and safe place. Then he goes into his recollection of this most recent of his testimonies: "The pangs of death surrounded me . . ." Then he switches to future tense saying, "For you will light my lamp . . . ," expressing his *hope* that he will see God's presence and faithfulness in the future. (He goes on about it at some length.) From there he goes back to a testimony and more praise to God, saying that this is what God *does:* "It is God who avenges me . . . delivers me from my enemies . . . gives me great deliverance."

Hear the hope in his words!

My own testimonies have the same effect on me. When I remind myself of them during any new battle or recall them in times of praise, they encourage me. They give me hope.

As I was reading Psalm 18, I saw David do what I, and so many others like me, have learned to do. When I saw it, I was struck by the thought that even thousands of years later, God has not changed. What was true of him then is still true now.

And *that* is the hope of the testimony, after all.

Today, remember on purpose.

> *"This I recall to my mind, therefore have I hope . . .*
> *Great is your faithfulness"* (Lamentations 3:21, 23).

Gabriel Shares a Testimony

Have you ever noticed that there was a testimony shared *by an angel* in the middle of the Christmas story—shared with obvious purpose?

Here's how it went: Gabriel shows up in Nazareth and appears to Mary, telling her, probably with some excitement (if angels get excited), that she's highly favored and God is with her. Mary obviously shows signs of fright, since Gabriel immediately follows with, "Don't be afraid, Mary! You have found favor with God!" Then he goes on to tell her about her upcoming role in bringing the savior to earth.

"How can this be?" Mary asks.

Not a rejection of the call; not disbelief; just a question. So Gabriel gives her the details of a miraculous conception, and then, almost as if to encourage her faith and create in her a vision and certitude of what is to come, he shares a testimony—a true story about God's miracle in the life of someone she knows.

"Now, indeed, your cousin Elisabeth has also conceived a son in her old age; and this is now the sixth month for her who was called barren. *For with God nothing will be impossible.*" There, Mary! Take hope from that story!

The theme of my book *Keepers of the Testimony* is that every testimony, our own or someone else's, is to be a carrier of hope. I have a precious notebook which chronicles many of my own testimonies of God's faithfulness from 1992 until today. Just a sentence or two for each is enough to bring a whole story to remembrance. Every New Years' Eve, or whenever I feel the need, I sit with a cup of tea and read those lists. I haven't forgotten the stories, but there's something about seeing them written down, listed in order, that gives definition to how consistent God's care really is.

Today, write down a God-story reminder, or read one.

"And not only so, but we glory in tribulations also: knowing that tribulation worketh patience; And patience, experience; and experience, hope. And hope maketh not ashamed" (Romans 5:3-5).

It Ain't Over

My husband is a sports enthusiast. Sometimes during a game when things are looking pretty bad for my husband's team, he'll say, "It ain't over till it's over," quoting Yogi Berra. Often, things eventually pick up and the game turns around. It's not that my husband is a hockey prophet. It's just that he can tell when the team is still in the game. If they are still fighting, there's hope. But if he can tell by the team's body language that they think it's over, he may even switch the channel. If *they* think it's over, then it is.

I like what my friend Reverend Peter Black wrote in a blog post entitled "Facing Giants." He suggested that neither negative circumstances nor bad reports should make us think we're defeated—that our game is over—when God is on our side.

Joseph didn't think his game was over, even though he sat in a prison for years. David might have thought it was over in Ziklag when his friends turned against him, blaming him when their families were captured by the enemy. But after shedding his own tears, David encouraged himself in the Lord and got back in the game.

And didn't Jesus look to win a great victory, even while carrying his cross to Golgotha?

In any challenging situation life brings, we can find hope in the many scriptures that tell us God is our strength and our victory.

- *"Although the fig tree shall not blossom . . . yet will I rejoice in the Lord . . . The Lord God is my strength, and he will make my feet like hinds feet, and he will make me to walk on my high places"* (Habakkuk 3:17,19).
- *"Rejoice not against me, O mine enemy: when I fall, I shall arise"* (Micah 7:8).
- *"I had fainted unless I had believed to see the goodness of God in the land of the living"* (Psalm 27:13).
- *"In all these things we are more than conquerors through him that loved us"* (Romans 8:37).

Today, think about that, and take heart.

ON RESTING ON THE ROCK

On a hill near our house in Shearstown, on the island of Newfoundland where I grew up, there was a big flat rock from which we could see for miles. It felt good to sit there on a breezy, sunny summer day and look at the world from a safe place.

The Solid Rock

The concept of trustworthiness is an easy one for us.

Sometimes we seem to know instinctively who or what to trust. A little child who jumps with abandon from the side of a pool into his mother's or father's arms seems to do it without thought or fear.

But not all children do that. Not all children know they have parents who will never let them fall. Maybe the ones who jump have learned whom they can trust.

Even a child will learn it.

But when we talk about trusting God, sometimes we get things mixed up. We think trust is something we offer to God. But it isn't an offering. It grows in us from what we learn of him.

We learn of his trustworthiness from his word, from what he has already done that shows his goodness and love and his unchanging nature and character. We learn of it from his faithfulness in our own lives and in the stories of his faithfulness in the lives of those around us.

If wrong ideas about God have stolen your ability to trust in him—your willingness to rest your whole life's weight on his word, his goodness and faithfulness—then go to the Psalms and let someone who knows him well tell you about him again.

Today, take another look.

"The Lord is my rock, and my fortress, and my deliverer; my God, my strength, in whom I will trust; my buckler, and the horn of my salvation, and my high tower. I will call upon the Lord, who is worthy to be praised: so shall I be saved from mine enemies" (Psalm 18:2, 3).

Live Here

Psalm 91 is one of my favorite psalms. True, this could be said of almost any of them, but I really do love this one. It talks about the "secret place" of safety provided for us under the shadow of the Almighty.

I've heard several sermons based on this scripture, and have been frustrated by the fact that the actual coordinates of the secret place seemed to be elusive. One pastor would say it was a place of constant prayer; another would say it was a place of unwavering obedience.

Somehow, whenever it was presented, I felt like that secret place was hard to find or, if I could manage to get there, it was a difficult position to maintain!

I would always take comfort, however, from verse two, which indicated something I felt I *could* do since it seemed to be more about him than about me. I could "say of the Lord, 'He is my refuge and my fortress; my God, in Him will I trust.'"

I knew I could say that because I knew him to be trustworthy.

But then, wouldn't a place of trust automatically become a place of prayer and obedience? Instead of being a means to enter into the secret place, prayer and obedience would spring from that place of safety and confidence close to our Father. Somehow, that just makes more sense to me.

Today, trust God.

> *"Oh, how great is your goodness which you have laid up for those who fear you, which you have prepared for those who **trust** in you in the presence of the sons of men! You shall hide them in the secret place of your presence from the plots of man. You shall keep them secretly in a pavilion from the strife of tongues"* (Psalm 31:19, 20).

The Secret Place

I just wrote about the secret place of Psalm 91, a place of trust in God.

If we let scripture explain itself, we'll see that both verse 2 of Psalm 91 and verse 19 of Psalm 31 indicate that trusting God puts us in a place apart from the evil found in this world. They mention plots of man, strife of tongues, the snare of fowler, pestilence, destruction and trouble.

It's all there, all the stuff we are afraid of.

And it seems we are hidden from it all when we're in that place of trust.

It's almost unbelievable; almost unfair.

So how does one find that place of trust?

Trusting God comes from knowledge of God—accurate knowledge. If we're having trouble trusting God then perhaps we have let misinformation about him sneak into our thinking.

Trust comes from experiencing God, too, and no one can teach us that.

In any case, let's go back every once in a while to Psalm 103 to check the state of our heart-picture of God. Millennia may have passed since this description was first spoken, but God hasn't changed.

No matter what we have learned or been told about him, this remains true.

Today, dare to believe it.

"I will set him on high because he has known my name" .
(Psalm 91:14b).

Fingerprints

I've not always had a tolerance for fingerprints.

Before I was married and had a home of my own, I often visited my sister Emmie on weekends, especially during the year I was teaching in a town near her. She had two small children and too much sense to waste her precious time looking for fingerprints on the coffee and end tables. I didn't have such good sense and attacked those fingerprints regularly, only to have them appear again within minutes. On one such occasion, Emmie laughed at me and said, "We'll see how dedicated you are to shiny furniture when you have sticky-fingered youngsters running around."

That was a long time ago. I have an appreciation for fingerprints now. I go looking for them these days, but for a different reason than I did back then.

Joel Osteen talked about it one day. He told how he had visited someone's home and had been unimpressed with a particular piece of art until the owner told him it had cost $1,000,000.

It was a Picasso.

It turns out the value of a painting is in who painted it—or, as Osteen said, " . . . whose fingerprints are on it."

Osteen used that story to say we are valuable because we are God's workmanship, created in Christ Jesus. God's fingerprints are all over us.

Every once in a while, and always late in December, I reflect on the year just past and look for God's fingerprints, evidence of his presence and involvement in my life. Although I've not had a year when I could say *every* print I found was God's, I *can* say I've seen evidence of his touch in every year. Just as he promised, he has never left or forsaken me—nor has he forsaken you. He never will.

Today, look for the fingerprints!

"I have covered thee in the shadow of my hand" (Isaiah 51:16).

Confidence

I had been watching with keen interest the campaigns being waged by the American Democrat and Republican presidential hopefuls. One phrase used often by the media pundits, analysts, spinners, et al. referred to the "confidence of the front runner."

The phrase was used in reference to the ability of the front runner to refrain from negative rhetoric against opponents, suggesting that those who expect to win don't just have a confident air about them; they can afford to be generous.

It occurs to me that everyone who calls on the name of the Lord ought to have that same confidence—that of one who knows his position is "overcomer".

If we have that kind of confidence, then we should also have the same generosity. Maybe that's why God tells us—expects us—to love our enemies and do good, not evil, to those who despitefully use us.

I'm sure there's more to God's instructions than I might seem to suggest here, but isn't it food for thought?

Trusting God will keep us from needing to be in strife with anyone.

After all, El Shaddai is our Father.

Today, just relax. And be nice!

"The Lord is the strength of my life; of whom shall I be afraid?"
(Psalm 27:1).

Carried

One lovely summer I vacationed at Disney World with my family. We spent most of our days at one of the Disney parks—Magic Kingdom, Epcot, Animal Kingdom, etc. It was fun and fabulous. Magical, even!

Late every evening, on the shuttle home, I saw something precious. After the heat and excitement of wonderful Walt Disney World, tired children were carried in their father's arms, most of the cherubs sleeping and completely oblivious to their surroundings. Some of them seemed cuddled and comfortable; others were simply splayed out (no other way to describe it), arms and legs hanging loose, completely supported by nothing but Daddy's strength.

Not one father looked wearied by his precious burden. Actually, they all looked happy. It could have been that they were happy to be leaving the park after all day, but it seemed to me they were *just happy*.

It made me wonder if when God says, "Be still and know that I am God," he's really saying, "Let me carry you now. You just rest."

We're told to walk by faith, and sometimes even to fight the good fight of faith. But even in the midst of the walk and the fight, there's a rest that comes from believing he's with us and in us and that he is our strength and victory.

And sometimes, because we're human, when we've fought the good fight and feel too tired even to walk, he will carry us.

Today, close your eyes for a minute and feel Abba's strength.

" . . . and underneath are the everlasting arms"
(Deuteronomy 33:27).

Time is Love

We all know how wonderful it is to be given the gift of time with those we love. And when someone we love takes time from a busy schedule to be with us, it just makes us happy. To know they delight in our presence as much as we do theirs—well, that's a joy beyond price.

That's the first thing I thought of recently when I read how Adam and Eve "heard the voice of the Lord God walking in the garden in the cool of the day" (Genesis 3:8). I thought of how happy they must have been there in that stunning beauty, with colors more vibrant and fragrances sweeter than we have ever known, with temperature perfect and breeze gentle.

I remembered God's reaction just after he had created them and blessed them, calling for fruitfulness and increase and giving them authority over the works of his hands in this home he had made just for them.

In my imagination, I saw him look around and smile, because it was all *very* good. And they were the joy of his heart.

And I wondered if this walk in the garden was a standing date they had—time to talk after the day was over, quality time between father and children. Love shared.

Abba still loves his children.

Today, listen for his voice and let him hear yours.

"My voice shalt thou hear in the morning, O Lord; in the morning will I direct my prayer unto thee and look up" (Psalm 5:3).

No Feelings

Remember when Jesus indicated that believing what he said brings joy and peace?

Well, on one more day of too-cold temperatures, I had a headache, a cough, and a multiplicity of sneezes—and my muscles ached and my hands and feet didn't want to warm up.

Not only that, but if I'd had enough hair to bad-mouth, I'd have said I was having a bad hair day.

Small stuff to complain about, you say, and you are so right! But my joy seemed to be buried under it all and wouldn't get up. My peace was intact, but not saying much.

But I knew they were there somewhere—both joy and peace—because I have faith: I believe God is who he says he is, and I am who he says I am.

It was a day to rest in that knowledge.

Joy would sing again, and peace would whisper, "All is well."

But that day, I decided to just eat my soup.

Today, don't worry about anything.

"There remaineth therefore a rest to the people of God"
(Hebrews 4:8-10).

New Adventure

One day I sat with a wonderful story-teller, Moira Brown of *100 Huntley Street*, and talked about the importance of stories.

As we discussed how our God-stories are supposed to give hope to the hearers and how that hope will motivate them to walk with God, I learned this lesson: No matter how much we think we are relying on the Lord as our help—even in something as simple as a television interview—we can get so involved in our own attempt to "get it done" that we forget where our true strength lies.

I enjoyed visiting with Moira—a consummate professional who creates heart warmth on the set under those bright lights—and as time went on it was easier to forget the cameras. Nevertheless, as I drove away from Crossroads Communications, I wished I had touched on *all* the talking points I had prepared. And I wished I had done a better job of following the instructions of the two publicists whose expertise was made available to me at The Word Guild's *Write! Canada* conference just a week earlier.

But eventually—sometime during my drive back home—I came to the conclusion that we have to rely on God to be the finisher of any work he gives us to do. That no matter how well I did or didn't do in that interview, *only God* could touch the hearts of *100 Huntley Street's* viewers. Only he could motivate and empower them to share their God-stories with their children and grandchildren.

Today, trust him and expect him to do his part.

> " . . . *showing to the generation to come the praises of the Lord,*
> *and his strength and his wonderful works that he hath done"*
> (Psalm 78:4).

ON TALKING TO GOD

I hate when I talk to someone and they keep looking over my shoulder.

God never does that.

Answered

He cried, "My God, My God, why have you forsaken me?"

That was Jesus on the cross, quoting Psalm 22.

In the psalm, David spent some time bemoaning his state. He was in trouble; people were mocking him and his trust in God; he felt weak, physically and emotionally. He cried out to God, saying God has made him trust since he was a small child.

"You have been my God, my strength!" David cries, almost as if he's wondering where God is now.

About two thirds of the way into the psalm, in the New King James Version, an interesting statement stands alone with no indication of why it is there:

"You have answered me."

From that point onward, David's voice changes. He no longer bemoans his present position and condition. Instead he turns to praise, and a sort of prophecy: "I will declare your name to my brethren . . . All the ends of the world shall remember and turn to the Lord . . . posterity shall serve him. It will be recounted of the Lord to the next generation; they will come and declare His righteousness to a people who will be born" (Psalm 22:22-31).

I realize this psalm of David is considered prophetic of Jesus' experience on the cross, but I can't help but think of one of my favorite verses from another psalm. Referring to the trusting one who is held in the secret place of God's presence, it says, "He shall call upon me and I will answer him" (Psalm 91:15).

Today, leave your place of prayer with assurance.

"Oh how great is Your goodness which You have laid up for those who fear you, which You have prepared for those who trust in You . . . You shall hide them in the secret place of Your presence from the plots of men"
(Psalm 31:19-20).

Before We Call

Our daughter was directing her first short film. An actor who played one of Glenn's and my favorite characters on the television show *NCIS* had agreed to play the lead role.

One morning, three days before the shoot was to start, I watched a talk show on television and heard a "name" actor tell how he obtained the lead role in a big film just four days before shooting started. When I heard it I decided, "I should tell Gillian that story next time we chat."

Later that morning, when I was on my way home from picking up groceries, I thought about the interview and hoped plans for Gillian's shoot were going well. She had been very busy with last minute preparations and was still waiting for the recreational vehicle that was a necessary part of the set. There had also been some concern that the short film schedule might conflict with that of *NCIS*. But the short film's lead actor, who played a key recurring role on *NCIS*, had been determined to make it work, so no one was too worried.

Suddenly, out of the blue, it occurred to me that Gillian had lost her lead.

When I got home there was a message on our phone from Gillian saying that—given his crazy schedule and the stress involved for him in trying to do everything—she had offered to release her one "name" actor from his commitment. Now she was waiting for a call from a possible pinch-hitter who turned out to be perfect for the role.

I called her back and told her about my morning. It reminded us both that God knows about every challenge that faces us.

Today, whatever happens, know that God isn't surprised.

> *"And it shall come to pass, that before they call, I will answer; and while they are yet speaking, I will hear"* (Isaiah 65:24).

The Farm

My father would often say to my mother after supper, "Come on, Louie. Let's go into the farm." They would hop in the truck and drive a few miles out of town to check out the fields where his crops were growing.

Even though he would have spent most of his day on the farm, there was something about seeing the fields at day's end—peaceful and green in the early dusk—that put a smile of satisfaction on my father's face.

Jesus talked about my father, or people like him. It's recorded in the book of Mark. "The kingdom of heaven is as if a man should scatter seed on the ground and should sleep by night and rise by day, and the seed should sprout and grow, he himself does not know how. For the earth yields crops by itself: first the blade, then the ear, then the full corn in the ear" (Mark 4:26-28).

If my father were writing this he would no doubt mention that he actually had to help the earth bring forth by sowing the seed, watering, weeding, and feeding. But he would also talk about the earth's miracle, I think, because he had respect for it. He knew that, without it, his own efforts would be fruitless. My father was grateful, though tired, at harvest time.

Answered prayers are sort of a harvest. The answers sometimes show up in much the same way vegetables do—first the blade, then the ear, and so on. I wonder if I ever get so used to looking at the various stages of growth before the final harvest comes that I forget the wonder and the mystery of its appearance. Forget that it started out as a prayer; forget that I'm looking at proof of God's faithfulness; forget to be thankful.

Today, let's remember past harvests.

> *"Herein is my father glorified, that ye bear much fruit;*
> *so shall ye be my disciples"* (John 15:8).

Moose and Deer and Bears, oh my!

My novelist friend and I were at the end of our east coast book tour. Before dawn on the day we left New Brunswick to return home we sat in the car getting ready to take on the last lap of our journey.

Suitcases; check! Books; check! Snacks and drinks; check! GPS set; check!

Donna looked over at me as she buckled up and said, "Pray for journeying mercies, Fay."

Part of my prayer was that the Lord would keep moose and deer off the highway, a concern especially since it was still dark and would be for another half hour or so.

At my "Amen," Donna insisted, "What about bears? Ask him to keep the bears away, too!"

Somewhat amused by this Southern Ontarian who thought she'd encounter bears on the highway in New Brunswick (I'd never in all my years running those eastern roads ever seen one), I nevertheless decided to humor her. I prayed again, " . . . and Lord, please keep the bears away!"

Not half an hour later and within a time span of about 15 minutes, we encountered two moose, two deer, and three black bears. Right there, near the side of the highway!

But not on it.

Today, ask for what you need.

"For he shall give his angels charge over thee" (Psalm 91:11).

On Grooves and Strongholds

The guest on *It's a New Day* was Dr. Terry Teykl, our pastor when we lived in Texas. I had always appreciated Dr. Teykl's ability to make the truth of the gospel something I could take home with me, something that would make a difference in the way I lived. His perspective was unique and his presentation always effective.

This time was no different. As I watched the interview, I was intrigued by his description of a stronghold, whether demonically influenced or not, as a groove made in our thought life—a groove which comes from thinking the same way over and over.

Dr. Teykl spoke at length about crafting prayers based on God's Word in order to create *divine* strongholds.

It made sense to me. I thought about marketers and publicists and television's "talking heads". They are obviously all about making a groove in our thinking that will influence what we buy, whom or what we vote for, or how we live in general.

As I listened, it occurred to me that creating divine strongholds in our children's thinking is what my book *Keepers of the Testimony* is about. As we tell our God-stories, making sure we incorporate the promise and the process as well as the proof of God's faithfulness, we are using a *God-given* tool to make those grooves.

That's what renewing of the mind is—allowing God's truth to form grooves. It is one way God will transform lives and destinies from a natural life-without-God existence into the purpose driven, joy-and-hope-and-faith-filled overcoming life God designed for every one of us.

Today, give God the opportunity to build strongholds in your mind by praying his promises and acknowledging his faithfulness.

"Be ye transformed by the renewing of your minds"
(Romans 12:2).

Virtual Prayer Room

It was another day listening to Dr. Terry Teykl on the television program *It's a New Day*.

His topic was, again, his passion: prayer. He talked about virtual prayer rooms, places online where people could ask for prayer or write their own prayer based on Bible promises and have others who log on agree with their prayer according to Matthew 18:19.

It sounded silly to me at first, but then I thought about how some people might be alone facing the tough things life throws at them, and how an on-line prayer room might be the only place they can connect with someone who will help bear their burden and so fulfill the law of Christ (Galatians 6:2).

As I listened, I remembered the simple prayers prayed at Aldersgate United Methodist Church where he was our pastor years ago, and the many wonderful proofs of God's presence, goodness, and faithfulness that came as a result of those prayers. Several of them were for me.

Dr Teykl's call to prayer in this way might seem small or strange to some, but consider this:

Something happened on a hillside long ago that probably seemed pretty small and strange to those watching, but look what Jesus did with a couple of little fish and some rolls!

Today, make way for a miracle!

"Again I say unto you, That if two of you agree on earth as touching anything that they shall ask, it shall be done for them of my Father which is in heaven" (Matthew 18:19).

The Phone Call

When I started writing my book *Keepers of the Testimony* in 2005, I began with the story of my two fourth grade students whom I referred to as my Texas Terrors.

Every time I worked on that chapter I cried. Every time! And I'd pray for Joshua, the boy the story was mostly about. He particularly touched my heart that year, perhaps because I knew that through no fault of his own there were circumstances in his life that could possibly make his road a difficult one.

"Lord, I call Josh to his destiny! If he's in trouble, let him cry out to you!" I prayed over and over as the days and the rewrites passed.

Once in a while I'd think it was a strange prayer, since I had no idea what his life was like. He might already be thriving on the right path, serving the Lord and raising little Texans. Nevertheless, tears and prayers poured out.

Years later, in February 2009, a phone call from Texas told me just what he'd been up to since fourth grade. I'd love for you to hear the whole story in his words as I did, but I'll just tell you this: When I started writing the book, Josh was in prison. He was there for three and a half years from age 19 to 23. Soon after he got out of prison he went back to his old ways, but a year later, on February 10, 2008, just a few days after *Keepers of the Testimony* was released, Josh fell to his knees in his apartment in Texas and cried out, "God, this is not who I am! You know my heart! If you love me, help me! Please save me!"

What joy to hear it!

Today, expect your prayers to be answered!

"The seed of the righteous will be delivered" (Proverbs 11:21).

"For he satisfies the longing soul and fills the hungry soul with goodness"
(Psalm 107:9).

Jesus Wept

Mary, Martha, and Lazarus were friends of Jesus—close friends. Often, they sat at Jesus' feet in their own home and listened to him teach. Maybe it was there that he told them, "If you will believe, you will see the glory of God" (John 11:40).

When Lazarus fell ill, his sisters immediately sent word to Jesus, confident that Jesus would come right away and heal their brother. They had heard about healings at his hand, and had probably seen it happen over and over—certainly enough to make them believers. There were those teachings, too. And, to clinch matters, he loved Lazarus!

But Jesus *on purpose* delayed his coming until Lazarus had died. Finally arriving on the scene, he wept.

I've often wondered why he wept. I can imagine why he delayed. To show them a greater miracle, maybe; to provide a prophetic action, as I've read; or to show that God is never in a hurry and does his work on his own time schedule. But why weep? He knew he was going to raise Lazarus, so surely he'd be thinking about the joy that was to come to his friends.

I wonder if he wept because, in his troubled spirit, he saw this scene repeated millions of times down through the years. He knew that for some reason or reasons that might elude us, there would be no miracle like the one Mary and Martha were about to see. He knew that even though he came to destroy the works of the enemy, death would still take its toll—too soon in many cases—until the wonderful day our last enemy would be destroyed.

But even though death must be allowed to cast it's shadow for a time, God has provided promises through which we can, here and now, partake of the divine nature—of life. And today, while Jesus weeps with those who weep, he is still ready to teach us when we sit at his feet.

> *"And Jesus, when he came out, saw much people,*
> *and was moved with compassion toward them,*
> *because they were as sheep not having a shepherd:*
> *and he began to teach them many things"* (Mark 6:33-35).

ON SOMETHING WE CAN'T EARN

Life's paradox: We like to think we deserve our stuff, and we're glad we don't get all we deserve.

The Gift

It is easy to focus on one truth so much that we overlook another.

In focusing on the important fact that seeds bear fruit in our lives—good fruit from good seeds and bad fruit from bad seeds (which is the reason it is so important to guard our hearts to ensure that good seeds remain and bad seeds are rooted out by the truth)—we can actually forget what the gospel is all about.

The gospel is about a gift.

Righteousness, which is simply our right standing with God, is not something we achieve by doing right. Impossible to earn, it was bought for us. We didn't have the ability to buy it 2000 years ago, and we still don't. Jesus bought it for us by taking the wages of our sin on himself and, in so doing, fulfilling the law and making the way for us to go free.

I must confess that the gift of righteousness is a concept I grapple with sometimes, perhaps because I know that even though I have received the blood-bought gift I can still make wrong choices, and I still live in a seedtime and harvest world.

But I also know that, when I ask, God is more than willing and able to redeem even my bad choices and root up bad seed. After all, he says his eyes are always on the righteous (Can you grasp that this means those who have been given the gift of righteousness?) and his ears open to our cry.

The one who planned our redemption waits for our cry, ready to teach us his ways, longing to bring us every good and perfect gift, by grace through faith.

Today, think of that when you pray!

> *"How shall he not with him [Jesus] also freely give us all things?"*
> (Romans 8:32)

The Armor

The afternoon speaker at church camp that year taught on the passage from Ephesians 6 which describes the armor of God the believer is to "take unto" himself.

One part of the armor was the breastplate of righteousness. The speaker said this righteousness was righteous living. His reason for holding this position was that unless one lives righteously, one is going to feel condemned and guilty. And that, he said, is no way to go into battle against the powers of darkness.

It made sense to me. I knew how guilt felt and it wasn't empowering. But still, something about it didn't sit right with me.

A full five years later, I lay in bed one night reading Ephesians. When I got to Chapter 6, I remembered what that man had said. Suddenly it hit me: He had to be wrong! I sat straight up in bed.

"It was God's armor!" I said.

Every other part of the armor came straight from God: truth, peace, faith, salvation, the word. All of them gifts. Surely, the righteousness that guards our heart in the midst of a battle *had* to be the righteousness Jesus bought for us. After all, hadn't the prophet Isaiah called *our own righteousness* "filthy rags"? Who would send a soldier into battle wearing filthy rags?

Not that right choices have no value. They bear good fruit, absolutely. But that night it became clear that the only true righteousness I would ever have, I would have to receive as a gift.

Today, walk around in the gift Jesus gave you.

"For if by one man's offence death reigned by one; much more they which receive abundance of grace and of the gift of righteousness shall reign in life by one, Jesus Christ" (Romans 5:16-18).

Who Deserves It?

Have you ever needed a favor from someone and wished you had done more for that person so that you would now be in a better position to ask?

Have you wished the same thing when you've asked God for favor?

The Old Testament stories indicate that the favor of God is earned. In those times, under a previous covenant, the favor of God was usually reserved for those who meticulously obeyed the laws. Obedience was an indication of fear of God, and God gave favor to those who feared him. The word translated "fear" would be probably more accurately translated "honor" or "respect", but the resulting obedience would be the same either way.

One day when I needed divine favor, it occurred to me that I didn't deserve it. Not a bit. My hope started to waver, but then I remembered: The law came through Moses but *grace* came through Jesus. Jesus changed everything! He wasn't just a good man who taught us how to live free. He bought the freedom for us, and said, "Here, this is for you."

"Freedom from what?" you might ask.

Freedom from everything you need freedom from, surely, and freedom from the need to earn his favor. Think about it: what could *you possibly do* that would put you in a better position than what *he did for you*?

How difficult it is for us to accept that! How we want to work for and deserve whatever good comes our way! Our culture demands that of us, doesn't it?

But *undeserved* favor was what I needed and that's what he offered me.

Today, just take a deep breath and think about what Jesus *really* did for you. Just breathe and believe, and receive with thanksgiving.

> *"For the law was given through Moses, but grace*
> *and truth came through Jesus Christ"* (John 1:17).

Perfection

I've often wondered why I consider perfection a worthy goal—why many of us do. Is it because our spirits know we came from perfection and want to return to it? Perhaps it feels like home to us.

During the Write! Canada conference, everyone mentioned that need to be perfect—called it a trap. Workshop leaders, continuing class leaders, and the plenary speaker all indicated that the pursuit of perfection can become debilitating. Not that we shouldn't use every means to be excellent, they said, but perfectionism is counter-productive. It can shut you down, if you let it, because nothing will ever be good enough for you.

Then workshop leader Ann Voskamp read the very first blog post she wrote. It was about her son bringing her a gift: he had carved a wooden spoon for her. She caressed the spoon in her hands as she read. "Is it perfect?" he had asked, "Will I make another one?" I won't do justice to her beautiful words, so I won't try, but at one point, after telling him it was perfect and that she wanted him to fill up the house with them, she held his small face in her hands and said, "You are perfect!"

As she spoke, I thought about how often I've heard it said that because of what Jesus did we're perfect in God's eyes. How often I think God must not see too well if he thinks I'm perfect! I'm forgiven and I have the gift of righteousness, but I'm not perfect. If I can see that, surely God can.

But then I saw something wonderful! Ann's little boy is not perfect in her eyes. *He is perfect in her heart!* As my daughter is not perfect in my eyes— she's too much like her parents for that! But she's perfect in our hearts, completely and always.

I get it now. My Father has eyes that see, but *I'm perfect in my Father's heart*. Surely, when I've done my very best, and my offering—the work of my hands—comes from *my* heart, then it, too, is perfect in his heart.

And, today, that's enough.

"While we were yet sinners, Christ died for us"
(Romans 5:8).

Safe at Home

I read a book called Soul Cravings, by Erwin Raphael McManus. The main theme of the book was the universal craving for connections, community, and family—for love, that "home" of the heart.

Jesus knew about our cravings. When asked which commandment was the most important he said, "You are to love God with all your heart and soul and strength." And then He added, "And you must love your neighbor as yourself."

Think of it! Who would *command* us to *give* what we most *crave*? Surely, someone who believes in sowing and reaping, as Jesus does!

But the kind of love Jesus is talking about doesn't originate with us. It starts with him. We've heard it since we were children: "We love him because he first loved us."

Loving God with all our heart can only be a response to his love. We recognize and receive his love, and we love back. It is only from that place of safety and fullness that we can freely love our neighbours.

As I read McManus' book, a song we used to sing when I was a child came to mind several times: "Jesus Keep me Near the Cross". It is from a vantage point close to the cross that I see God's love in action. Whenever I stop feeling the love, I run back there. In that bloody scene I see what love submitted to, and I dare to believe it was on my behalf. I feel valued and wanted.

And I am safe at home.

Today, be safe.

"For God so loved the world, that he gave his only begotten son,
that whosoever believeth in him should not perish but have everlasting life"
(John 3:16).

The Mercy of God

I'm so glad that David, the shepherd who became king, wrote Psalm 103.

In this song of praise and thanksgiving he's talking to himself, to his soul—his mind, will, and emotion—about what God has done and, in fact, still does for him.

I wonder if he's encouraging himself in the Lord here, too, like when his wives and children and the wives and children of all his fighting men were captured by their enemies at Ziklag.

Somehow that thought encourages *me*.

In listening to David, I realize that it is okay—in fact, necessary—that I remind myself of God's track record of mercy. In Psalm 103:10 David remembers "he has not dealt with us according to our sins, nor punished us according to our iniquities."

That's talking about us, too!

Today, let's focus for a while on what his mercy has already brought, and continues to bring.

> *"But the mercy of God is from everlasting to everlasting"*
> (Psalm 103:17).

Forgotten Rest

When Jeremiah brought the word of the Lord to the children of Israel (whose shepherds had led them astray) he said about them, "They have forgotten their resting place. All who found them devoured them."

Such sad words! It wasn't that they didn't have a resting place. They had forgotten it.

The place of rest for the children of Israel was in trusting God and, in trusting, following his instructions. There was *both* rest *and* safety in that.

I wonder if they had just forgotten their place of rest in the sense of neglecting it. Or had they lost their way and couldn't find their way back, or perhaps forgotten it ever existed?

Whichever, it is a lesson for us.

The writer of Hebrews said that we who have believed in Jesus have entered into rest; but sometimes we fall short of it through unbelief. What is interesting is that shortly after saying those things, he adds, "he that has entered rest has *ceased from his own works.*"

Simple isn't it? We can't be working and resting at the same time.

We can rest because Jesus did the work for us, fulfilling the law and giving us the gift of righteousness.

Words worth considering today: gift, righteousness, trust, enter, rest.

"Come unto me all you who are burdened and heavy laden and I will give you rest" (Matthew 11:28).

True Love

A few words—not my own—about true love:

God loves you so much that he gave his only begotten son, so that you should believe in him and not perish but have eternal life, starting right now! The Father loves you just as he loves Jesus, and will with him freely give you all things that pertain to life and godliness.

As the Father loves you, so does Jesus! Greater love has no man than this, that he should lay down his life for his friends. He has loved you with an everlasting love and will never leave you or forsake you. He will be with you always. He even promised that you will live with him, someday, in a beautiful home he has especially prepared.

Who shall separate you from the love of Christ? Shall tribulation or distress? Shall persecution or famine, or nakedness or peril or sword?

No, never! In all these things you are more than conquerors through him who loved you!

You can be sure that nothing—neither anything in this life, nor death, nor angels, nor principalities, nor powers, nor things happening now, nor things that might yet come, nor height nor depth, nor any creature—shall be able to separate you from the love of God which is in Christ Jesus your Lord.

His love motivates his every thought toward you, because you are precious in his sight.

Today, just believe that and relax!

"I have loved thee with an everlasting love: therefore with loving kindness have I drawn thee" (Jeremiah 31:2-4).

ON LIVING THE PLAN

There's a way that seems right unto man, but it isn't.

God has ways that are right.

Caleb Got It

My Bible fell apart today. I don't expect them to last forever, but I'm a note-making Bible owner, and I hate to have those things I've written on the pages relegated to obscurity in the wilderness that is my bookshelf.

So here's a wealth of wisdom I found on one page. Sorry, I can't credit it. I've long since forgotten who said it:

Caleb—

- Was willing to be different. (He said yes when five million said no.)
- Stood up to naysayers. (Even when he was in the minority.)
- Connected with others of like mind.
- Was fully obedient, not selectively so.
- Was ready for adventure.
- Believed he was a winner.
- Had no fear of obstacles. ("Give me that mountain!")
- Patiently waited for his time.
- Was prepared to seize the moment.
- Didn't give up; he made it to the Promised Land.

Also, he didn't equate ease with safety.

Today, take up the challenge and take some land.

"And Caleb stilled the people before Moses, and said, Let us go up at once,
and possess it; for we are well able to overcome it"
(Numbers 13:29-31).

Give me that Mountain

I'm not old. Not really.

That said, I'll admit that sometimes, given today's culture of youth, even someone of my tender age might begin to *think* old. By that, I mean one might begin to coast—to retire when one should re-fire.

Lately, I admit, I've been looking longingly at coasting. It crept up on me slowly, I think, but I realized it when my husband and I were presented with a possible opportunity, a challenge that would take a fair bit of courage and stamina.

It looked like just too much trouble!

But then I read a blog by my friend, author Mary Haskett. She pointed out that while one is still living and breathing there is never a time to stop doing.

I guess I shouldn't even think about coasting at this age, and probably not any time soon.

So, just for inspiration, I'll hunt for stories about people who have *taken* a mountain while others rocked on their porch, *talking about* the mountain.

Today, let's learn from Caleb—and act like Caleb.

> " . . . *and now, lo, I am this day four score and five years old . . . therefore give me this mountain whereof the lord spake in that day . . . if so be the Lord will be with me, I will be able to drive them [the Anakims] out, as the Lord said"* (Joshua 14: 10-11).

Surprising Connections

Hands *do* something.

While they are no doubt created for many purposes, one purpose of hands is work, the accomplishment of *something*.

Most societies grade accomplishment high on the value scale. They consider unwillingness to work much less than admirable. In Old Testament times, having profitable work and enjoying its fruit was considered to be part of the blessing. In New Testament times, if one refused to work, he didn't eat!

In an article entitled "The Most Regrettable Failure", published in *Beyond Ordinary Living Magazine,* I wrote about something that kept my hands from work. Fear of failure—more accurately fear of wasting time—kept me from attempting to write my first book, and did so for quite some time!

I'm still surprised that it took me so long to figure out what was going on, but I'm glad I finally did. Realizing that fear was my problem—and that fear is a dastardly thief—gave me enough stubborn fortitude to sit at the computer and pound out sentence number one.

This morning, as I read this verse in Zechariah, I saw again the strong connection between fear and lack of willingness to work.

Today, read the context of this verse to see more fully what was going on, and why they need not fear. Why *we* need not fear.

"Fear not, but let your hands be strong"
(Zechariah 8:13).

The Most Regrettable Failure

I just wrote about how fear of failure almost kept me from writing my first book. As I mentioned, my fear of failure was rooted in fear of lost time.

I was afraid of trying anything—like writing a book—that would take months or years. If I failed, it would mean I had wasted much of the precious time God had given me on this earth. Therefore, because I felt responsible to use my time wisely, I attempted only those things I felt I could do successfully.

For years, fear stole the very thing it promised to protect—my time.

Fear of failure doesn't always look the same. It morphs into different shapes with different people. Some are afraid to fail because of what people will think or say. Others are afraid of losing money in failed ventures.

Fear produces its own reason.

I realize that what some might *think* is fear is really just prudence. However, those of us who are, or have ever been, under the influence of debilitating fear know it isn't prudence. Somehow, deep inside, we know it. We might not know exactly what the problem is, but we know it's a problem, not prudence.

None of us want to fail at anything. That's just natural. But the most regrettable failure just might be the failure to try.

Today, let's not be afraid of what God has put in our heart to do.

*"What time I am **afraid**, I will trust in thee"*
(Psalm 56:2-4).

Significance

If there is anything the story of the one lost sheep makes clear it is this: Every life is important to God. Performance of any kind is not a prerequisite for significance to him.

But we are made in our Father's image and, therefore, deep down we all want to be part of significant productivity. It's in our spiritual DNA. So just for today, let's define significance in terms of work—"doing something that is of benefit to the generation in which we live, and perhaps even beyond."

Here are four examples of significance. Two of these people influenced generations because of only one event. One never knew how significant he was.

- Runaway Moses eventually led a race of people out of slavery and to the doorstep of their homeland.
- Young David, shepherd and song-writer, freed his countrymen from a terrifying enemy; then, after years of persecution, he became king and expanded the territory of his people through war.
- Rahab was known primarily as a harlot until, in one act of faithful obedience and undeniable strength of mind and courage of heart, she saved her whole family from destruction.
- Bartimaeus is remembered for one day in his life when his persistence attracted the attention of Jesus. In the millennia since then, millions have read his story and found their own courage because of it.

In the lives just mentioned we see that trusting and obeying God—and in some way reflecting his character—were part of their accomplishing something of lasting significance. So perhaps we don't need to know *how* to be significant, or even work to be significant. We just need to trust and obey.

Today, let's do that.

"For the Lord God will help me; therefore I shall not be confounded: therefore I have set my face like flint, and I know that I shall not be ashamed"
(Isaiah 50:7).

Look in your Hand

The visiting preacher talked about reasons one might get "stuck" as in the mud. More importantly, he gave a way to get unstuck: Use what is in your hand.

As I listened, I thought of the shepherd boy who came upon some Israeli soldiers facing Goliath. They were definitely stuck, and if *they* remained stuck so would he.

Not once do we see David accepting excuses for the situation—although there was one mighty big excuse! We don't see him taking a back seat either—afraid to hurt his brothers' feelings or concerned about their opinion if he stepped up to the challenge when they had failed to do so. He didn't even ask God if it was his will that he fight Goliath, or ask him to give Goliath into his hand.

David knew his covenant and had experienced its blessing on the hillside as he cared for his father's sheep. He knew what God's plan for his enemies was, so he didn't need to pray about this giant. He just stepped up and volunteered, persuading the king to let him go by telling him the stories about the sheep-stealers on the hillside. The stories worked. Before long, after turning down King Saul's not-in-use armor, David ran to Goliath with a rough wooden slingshot and five smooth stones. That's all any onlooker would have seen, at least.

Can you imagine what the others thought as they watched him go? "What a crazy kid! How arrogant—or stupid, more likely!"

Just stones and a slingshot, but they brought him to a throne. When he used them, that is.

Today, look at what's in your hand.

"And the LORD said unto Joshua, Stretch out the spear that is in thy hand toward Ai; for I will give it into thine hand. And Joshua stretched out the spear that he had in his hand toward the city" (Joshua 8:18).

Is it I, Lord?

I attended a funeral mass for my friend's mother. Only the fifth time I had ever attended a Roman Catholic Church service, I was impressed again with the beautiful music and lyrics. I was moved by one song enough to write it on the back of my check book. Written by Daniel L. Schutte, 1981, it is based on Isaiah 6, in answer to: "Whom will I send?"

> "Here I am Lord. Is it I, Lord?
>
> I have heard you calling in the night.
>
> I will go, Lord, if you lead me.
>
> I will hold your people in my heart."

This song probably affected me so much because I had recently spent three days with over two hundred writers who are Christian, all of whom would identify with the songwriter's need to be led.

The songwriter talks about a calling in the night—referring, no doubt, to Samuel's call from God.

Our call may come at any time our hearts are open to listen. Sometimes, the call is to follow a path we've already identified, or to show a new road to take. Sometimes the night-calling is merely to trust, to believe, and to let go of fear.

No matter what or when the call, the mystery of the voice and, indeed, just the hearing of it, is precious. Responding to it brings only joy.

Today, if you hear the call, don't be afraid to answer.

"And the LORD came, and stood, and called as at other times, Samuel, Samuel. Then Samuel answered, Speak; for thy servant heareth"
(1 Samuel 3:10).

Breakfast with Jean

As I finished my cup of tea that morning, I watched Jean Vanier on television. It was one of those programs where Mr. Vanier—humanitarian, philosopher and founder of L'Arche homes and programs dedicated to the support of people who have intellectual disabilities—is speaking to someone off camera. The mesmerizing one-sided conversation rambles as the camera leaves at one point and picks up at another. As he often does, Jean Vanier talked about love and value.

He said we give people value by how we look at them, listen to them, or touch them. If you have ever found yourself in conversation with someone who continually looks over your shoulder, or if you have had your hand hurriedly shaken in church by someone who didn't take the time to look at your face—as if there was some quota to be met—you know Jean Vanier is right.

As I listened, I thought about the many ways we devalue people, deliberately or otherwise. Maybe we become unavailable because we are so busy, or maybe we've been hurt and withdraw for a while. For whatever reason, we don't chat with them as freely as we used to, don't look at them as we pass by them in church or at work, don't call or e-mail as often. Our actions say, even if our hearts don't, "You aren't valuable to me anymore."

God doesn't ever do that. He is the very *source* of true love. Listen to just a little of what he says:

- "I will *never* leave you or forsake you" (Hebrews 13:5).
- "*Come unto me* all you who are weary and heavy laden, and I will give you rest" (Matthew 11:28).
- "I will [continually] guide you with my eye" (Psalm 32:8).
- "I have loved you with an *everlasting* love; therefore with loving kindness I have drawn [pursued] you" (Jeremiah 31:3).

Today, think about how he values you. Think about the cross.

Rooted

I've had good success with my annuals this year because I finally got it: annuals are finicky plants that need constant attention! They need fertilizer regularly, and water even more regularly. The roots aren't very deep and can quickly dry out in hot weather. In fact, unless the natural conditions are perfect, these little ones can get into trouble and wilt and die in very short order.

Trees aren't like that. I've decided that we were designed to be like trees, not flowers. Aren't we called "trees of righteousness, the planting of the Lord?" When the tree's roots go deep as they should, they nourish and water the tree even when conditions fluctuate around them. In the same way, when our roots go deep in the assurance of God's love, we thrive.

When *they* don't, *we* don't.

Come to think of it, if we aren't assured of God's love, it's impossible to love him the way we should. And we definitely won't love our neighbors as ourselves! Oh, we might like our sweet neighbors, but there's no love lost between us and the ornery ones!

Isn't it interesting that everything in Christianity starts with God? Human religion starts with humans. In man-built religion we live well in order to receive favor from whatever god we hope to impress. But Christianity isn't like that. The Bible tells us that God loves first and gives first.

1 John 4:19 says, "We love him because he first loved us."

From that place of peace and safety and value, we find love to give back, and to give out. And we thrive, like well-rooted trees.

Today, know you are loved. And rest.

"For this cause I pray, . . . that Christ may dwell in your hearts by faith; that you being rooted and grounded in love, may be able to comprehend with all the saints what is the breadth and depth and height and to know the love of Christ . . . that you might be filled with all the fullness of God"
(Ephesians 3: 14-19).

My Favorite F's

I had breakfast with friends one morning. My friend Sharon had just got back from a backpacking trip in Vietnam with her daughter. She regaled us with stories, sharing pictures to back them up. (I wouldn't have considered Sharon to be the most adventurous girl in the world, although she has been known to hold a snake in Sunday school—a snake owned by Gail, another of the breakfast buddies.)

That morning another friend, Linda, brought along the magazine, *Beyond Ordinary Living,* which sported a full page picture of her and "Little Linda" and the article that she had written about the first time they met. Well past fifty, Linda is on her way to a new career in writing.

So I got to thinking about words like fifty**,** feisty, and fabulous.

There's quite a list of fabulous feisty people in my life. Here are just a few: Mary became a published author at seventy; Linda and Jerry retired and built Shiloh Place on their beautiful country property, a home just for missionaries who need a place to crash and rest; my feisty friend Jill recently endured a nasty major operation and a few days later was out getting her hair and nails done because she refused to have life altered by that horrific experience; Diann is a decade beyond fifty and still empowering women with her conferences and making great waves of difference far beyond that venue; Aunt Anne started her undergraduate degree when she was fifty, finished her PhD when she was sixty-seven, and quit teaching at Rutgers University when she was eighty-something; and finally my mother, Louie, who—four decades past fifty—inspires me with her ready humour and forceful opinions.

Today, whatever your age, be fabulous! The Lord approves and enables.

*"Those that be planted in the house of the Lord shall **flourish** in the courts of our God. They shall still bring forth **fruit** in old age;*
*[that old age is **future** for us!] they shall be **fat** and **flourishing;***
to show that the Lord is upright: he is my rock and there is no
unrighteousness in him" (Psalm 92:12-15).

Flying High

I figured if God wanted us to fly he'd have given us wings.

But then I heard someone talk about the natural laws of flying. He said that a 747 would have flown when Jesus walked on earth if only someone had figured out how the laws worked. For some reason, that changed things for me, and flying has become much more comfortable.

Although, there *are* those delays!

But delays and late luggage aside, if there's anything I've learned about flying—and life!—in the last few years it is this: Face your fears and don't give in to them.

I'm not talking about rejecting prudence, which is seeing the danger and hiding from it. What I am talking about is when you know what "the plan" is but you are just too afraid to follow it.

Here's what I mean: If Peter hadn't walked on the water, if Moses hadn't stepped into the Red Sea, or if David hadn't faced Goliath, it would have been fear that stopped them, not prudence. Because they all had God's Word, his direction, on what they should do, it would have been fear that kept them from following it.

But what joys, what deliverance, what victories they would have missed! (Not to mention what truth about God—and what inspiration—we would have missed!)

I think they would all tell us that living above fear is not just the way we were designed to live; it's also just plain fun. It's where we'll find our highest joy.

Today, let's follow the plan!

"For God hath not given us the spirit of fear; but of power, and of love, and of a sound mind" (2 Timothy1: 6-8).

Legacy

There was a note on a "writers' list-serve" recently from a young man who has a story to tell, a distinct voice, and the heart to get both on paper and out into the world. The note referred to the scripture which talks about us having "threescore years and ten".

Mind you, I think that scripture's reckoning of years was specific to the wilderness travelers who had refused to enter the promise land, so I'm not too concerned about it at my tender age. But point taken: We aren't here forever.

Then he noted something that the psalmist said repeatedly, " . . . establish the work of our hands for us."

It sounds almost desperate. Time is going by too quickly and he feels an urgency to accomplish something of importance.

I get that. I remember a few years ago when my mortality took on a more pronounced reality. I looked back over my life and wondered why I hadn't even tried to do what had been in my heart to do—to write my first book. After a while I recognized the nudges I was getting in that direction, and took action. Now, as I see a few more wrinkles show up, I'm in an even greater hurry to get "words" out there, eager to give something to another generation.

That makes sense, too, because we're made in the image of a Creator and a Giver.

As for my young friend, when I read his note I was happy to see that he has already learned that our ability to leave something good behind is found in the very same source from whom springs the desire. God calls us to the work and provides what is needed.

Today, whatever you are called to do, know the work is not yours alone.

"And let the beauty of the LORD our God be upon us: and establish thou the work of our hands upon us; yea, the work of our hands establish thou it"
(Psalm 90:16-17).

Over to you, Lord.

It may sound flippant at first hearing, but this phrase, "Over to you, Lord," which I picked up from my friend's blog (maryhaskett.com), has become almost a mantra for me.

It is not about doing nothing. Our righteousness has been bought and paid for, but we are called to a life of productivity. Even when we have entered into the rest of God, we still have work to do.

The phrase is just a way of saying, "God, I'm doing my part, whatever it is, but I know you are my strength—and not just emotional or physical strength. You are the power behind what I do; you make it work. When I am successful, I know that although my hands and feet and mind and voice were involved, the work started and ended with you."

It also says, "I refuse to worry about this problem or challenge. I will enjoy this day and the work you have given and will trust that you are to me just who you said you'd be."

Today, do what you know to do and then say, "Over to you, Lord."

"We then, as workers together with him, beseech you also that ye receive not the grace of God in vain" (2 Corinthians 6:1).

ON GETTING IT RIGHT

If at first you don't succeed, read the creator's manual.

Adjustments

My shoulder pain finally got to me. I'd been ignoring it for ages; after all, I thought, shouldn't I expect my body to fall apart as the years get behind me?

Then I woke up and realized that I expect to have a whole lot of years ahead of me too, and I surely don't want to spend them in pain. I became very motivated to change something. I wasn't sure what, but something had to give!

So I just left Dr. Scott's office armed with an exercise plan and a sheet showing me how to establish an ergonomically correct relationship with my computer. With the help of books to lift the monitor, more books for a footrest, a lifted seat and lowered armrests, I'm good to go.

Why, oh why, didn't I do this long ago?

And why, oh why, when life doesn't go the way the manufacturer says it should, don't we go to the life manual to find out what adjustments we should make? Why do we think we have it all figured out and assume we couldn't possibly need to change?

Realignment of our hearts and minds might be in order!

In fact, daily comparison with the manual might help us to stay spiritually and mentally ergonomically correct.

Today, let's get realigned! It feels good!

"I am come that they might have life and that they might have it more abundantly" (John 10:10).

Insider Information

Many scriptures talk about the blessings that come to those who trust in the Lord. Some might think of those blessings as a reward for trust, sort of like God is saying, "Okay, let's watch and see if they trust me. If they do I'll send this . . . whatever."

Somehow, I don't think that's why or how the blessings associated with trust come. I think it might be something of a Warren Buffet phenomenon.

A guru to the business world, Mr. Warren Buffet is sought after by business schools all over the world to provide opportunity for their students to "sit at his feet" and learn, even if for just an hour. He may benevolently try to give those students the benefit of his experience, but the good that would come to them from it wouldn't be his reward for their attention; it would be the result of their following through on what he said. To have his advice would be invaluable to any students who would trust him enough to act on it. On the other hand, it would be useless to anyone who wouldn't.

In the same way, if we trust God we'll do what he says. Following his instruction will eventually bring the good he intends.

Here's just one simple example: The Bible tells us not to be drunk with wine, wherein is excess. Imagine if no one, anywhere, was ever drunk with wine. There would never be a broken-hearted parent whose child was killed by a drunk driver. No children left fatherless by a disease associated with alcohol. No families living in fear of a father and husband who returns, violent, from a binge. The good in our world that would come from following just one of God's instructions is easily identifiable.

While our eternal salvation has been bought and paid for and is freely given, not earned but received by faith, *the life we live on earth is, to a great degree, connected to our choices*. We'll make good ones if we trust the insider information sitting right there on our night table!

Today, listening up just might be the smartest thing we ever do.

"Thy word is a lamp unto my feet and a light unto my path"
(Psalm 19:105).

Reward or Result

There was a wealthy man who owned a beautiful and prospering orchard. This man was old and about to die. Knowing his sons were lazy and might starve if left to care for the orchard themselves, he told them he had a fortune buried under the trees, and it was theirs if they could find it.

The man died that winter, and his sons did exactly what he had hoped they would. In the spring they began to dig, searching for the gold. Through the summer they dug and into the fall. On sunny days they dug, and even sometimes in the rain. As the days grew crisp, the young men, tanned and strong, looked at each other in frustration and said, "Where is this gold our father promised? It surely is not here!"

One looked up into the trees and saw the golden canopy above them. There were countless beautiful golden peaches and apples hanging from the branches. "Aha! There!" he cried. "Our wise father knew our wealth was in the orchard!" The brothers sold their bountiful harvest and enjoyed the wealth, good health, and now the wisdom their father wanted them to have all along.

Some years ago, a relatively new believer told me about his own "Aha!" moment. He said, "I think I know why the wisdom of God carries riches and honor and long life in her hands. I used to think God rewarded us with them if we feared him, but now I think it's that if we follow God's wisdom, we know the right thing to do. It is doing the right thing that brings all of those other things! They aren't the *reward* of wisdom; they're the *result* of it!"

We may not immediately see the good results of *"think on things that are pure"*, *"forgive, as you are forgiven"*, *"guard your heart for out of it come the issues of life"*, *"let not these words depart from your mouth, but meditate on them night and day"*, or *"when you ask, believe you receive"*, but the benefits are real.

"And unto man he said, Behold, the fear of the LORD, that is wisdom; and to depart from evil is understanding" (Job 28:27-28).

Thanks Boss

Whenever Special Agent Anthony DeNozo of *NCIS* fame says, or does, something stupid, his boss, Special Agent Jethro Gibbs, smacks him up the side of the head. DeNozo says, "Thanks, Boss," every time.

One April morning I received a figurative smack up the side of my head. As I sat in my front room—with my cat, Casey, painstakingly grooming himself on the chair beneath the window—I read the Beatitudes chapter, Luke 6.

For some reason I have always read the Beatitudes as separate statements, but that morning I saw something else going on.

Jesus has just come through a rough patch. On the one hand, it's been great—multitudes hanging on his every word and every day bringing healings and miracles. And he's just selected an amazing group of guys, all of them eager to be his helpers and students, his disciples.

On the other hand, he's had people on his case at just about every turn: "Why did you heal that woman *here* and *now*? How can you say *that*? What makes you think you have the right to eat *that*? And drink with *those* people?" On and on!

He'd better warn his new disciples about how to deal with this stuff because he knows what they're like. The more gregarious of them want to be liked, looked up to, popular, wanted. They love the multitudes. Others, the quiet ones, love him but would very much like to stay under the radar.

He'd better let them know that *whatever it is they like* is not going to happen *everywhere* and with *everyone*. He'd also better tell them how to deal with it. After all, a couple of them might decide it'd be fun to put their persecutors on an island and nuke them, or call fire down from Heaven on them, and *that's* not of the right spirit, for sure!

He finds a good level place to stand and calls them around.

"Okay, guys, here's the thing: If you're mistreated or end up poor, hungry, or crying because people despise you or are afraid of you, thinking you're naïve or, worse, dangerous because you believe what I say—and trust me, some of it will happen—cheer up!

Be happy because you're blessed.

You're blessed because you're living on the only solid rock there is. In fact, you're setting yourself up to receive great reward—not because they're angry at you but because you've found the right path.

But hear this: if you sell the truth for the sake of position, wealth, or being widely accepted, or if you hide your faith or let up a bit on 'following' in order to get those things, you're really in trouble, because you're building your life on shaky ground. You hear what I'm saying?"

Okay, Jesus, we understand that there's no way we're going to avoid making people mad at us if we follow you!

"Good, but this is important: Make sure you don't return the persecution! Do good to the persecutors—find something good to say about them, and find ways to be kind to them. Just treat them the way you'd like to be treated. Don't spend your time judging or condemning them. I didn't come to do that, and I don't want you doing it either. Don't forget what I taught you about sowing and reaping. It works *all* the time. After all, if you *act* like them you *are* like them, and you'll end up being blind while trying to lead the blind. No good comes from that, ever! So get rid of that speck in your eye—that desire to persecute those who hate you. Trust me in this: it's the only way you can do any good—the *only* way."

Yes, Boss.

"And by the way, that goes for how you treat each other, too. Got that?"

Yes, Boss. Thanks, Boss.

Today, let's listen to the boss.

"*. . . freely ye have received, freely give*" (Matthew 10:7-9).

Godlessness

A picture comes to mind of an actress who accepted an award and commented scornfully that Jesus definitely *hadn't* helped her get it.

None of us doubted it, did we?

That's probably unkind. It *is* unkind.

Jesus loves her, even though she made me angry. But sometimes it seems the media moguls and some of the stars of the entertainment world are bent on pushing the notion that to follow a biblical lifestyle is not only outmoded and naïve, it's downright dangerous to the wellbeing of the rest of the world. Their words and actions show they want God *out*!

But let's bring it home. Do *we* ever live godlessly?

When we face our days, our challenges or our decisions, as if we are alone; when we live life without bringing into the equation what God has said about what is going on; or when we live without hope in any situation, aren't we living godlessly?

Selah.

May we not live godlessly for even one moment!

After all, we don't need to—not ever.

Let today be God-filled.

"Now the God of hope fill you with all joy and peace in believing, that you may abound in hope, through the power of the Holy Ghost" (Romans 15:13).

On a Clear Day

Jesus said this about our eyes: *"The light of the body is the eye; therefore when thine eye is single, thy whole body is full of light"* (Luke 11:34).

For years, that statement was beyond me. I'd wonder, *When is my eye single and how does my body get to be full of light?* I knew its meaning wasn't as literal as that might make it sound, but still, I didn't get it.

Since then, I've decided that what is important is my understanding of its *application*. A single eye is a focused eye, and when my eye is focused on the things of the light—of truth—it affects everything about my life. The way I keep my eye single is by giving due respect to its function and choosing well where I look.

Here are just a few Bible admonitions about "looking":

- To Lot's wife: "Do not look behind you" (Genesis 19:17).
- "Let thine eyes look straight ahead. Ponder the path of your feet" (Proverbs 4:25, 26).
- "Look unto the rock from which you are hewn" (Isaiah 51:1).
- "Look unto me and be ye saved" (Isaiah 45:22).
- "We look not at the things which are seen, but the things that are unseen" (2 Corinthians 4:18).
- "Unto them that look for him shall he appear" (Hebrews 9;28).
- "Looking unto Jesus, the author and finisher of our faith" (Hebrews 12:2).

It doesn't matter how many or few scriptures about "looking" we find. What really matters is the overall biblical truth about where we keep our inner eyes, the eyes of our heart.

Today, as that chorus of my childhood went, " . . . be careful little eyes what you see."

"They looked to Him and were radiant,
and their faces were not ashamed" (Psalm 43:5).

The Book

The book of Malachi tells an interesting story.

God's chosen people had experienced some troubles and they'd been running off at the mouth over it. They'd been saying, "It doesn't make any difference whether you honor God or not. The wicked are doing pretty well, and we aren't. By their actions they tempt God, and yet they go free!"

In doing this, said Malachi, they spoke evil of God and despised his words. They looked at God's commandments as weariness, not wisdom. Then, while trying to appear righteous, they chose their own way by giving the dregs to God as offerings.

All because they became offended when they saw the wicked prosper.

But God loved them anyway, and honoured his promise to their fathers by sending his prophet to tell them how they could turn things around—because *they* were the ones who would have to do it. They would have to return to him, in *heart* and word and deed, and leave the wicked to him.

As New Covenant believers we know our favor comes by the blood of Jesus, shed in love to set us free from the law of sin and death. It's all grace and we know it, but we still need to guard our thoughts and words—if for no other reason than he's told us how creative our words are!

It's interesting that the book of Malachi says a "book of remembrance" is being written, not of the words of the wicked, but of those who fear and honor God.

"'And they shall be mine' says the Lord of hosts" (Malachi 3:17).

Today, let's fill up the book with good words.

"Then those who feared the Lord spoke to one another, And the Lord listened and heard them, So a book of remembrance was written before Him For those who fear the Lord and meditate on His name" (Malachi 3:16,17).

Context

I was at our monthly ladies' breakfast. A very relaxed and unstructured event, the breakfast date has been going on for several years and is one of the highlights of my month. Good food, good stories, good friends.

There were just five of us that morning, and we resumed the Bible study that we had set aside for over a year. We had missed it, and were excited as we looked at the first chapter of Ephesians.

One member of our group had done a comprehensive study of Ephesians in the past. She mentioned that the first three chapters of the book establish our position, i.e. *how we got to be who we are*. The rest of the book seems to say, "Therefore, *because of who you are, do this, because you can*!"

They were exciting connections:

- Do it, because you can.
- You can, because of who you are.

The book has just a few chapters.

Today, why not read them at one sitting and see what they're saying to you.

"I, therefore, the prisoner of the Lord beseech you that ye walk worthy of the vocation of which you are called"
(Ephesians 4:1).

Moderation

That morning, my 20696th, if my lazily utilized math skills served well, I woke up and smelled the coffee, and had a mug of same—with a side order of guilt because just the day before I had told the readers of my blog that I had given it up.

My husband said, "What are you going to do with this, given that you said you'd given up coffee?"

Confess to my readers, of course—which I did.

I enjoyed my coffee-mug-up that morning, but I can't indulge every morning. I don't enjoy the painful joints that I would end up with if I gave in to my taste-buds' demands—especially since my enjoyment of one steaming mug of full-flavored robust jump-start generally leads to a second or even a third if it's a slow morning and I'm sitting at the computer.

I guess enjoyment of life calls for some boundaries.

Boundaries are often looked at as enemies, but they aren't always. Often they are friends.

As a form of boundary, moderation has a beauty all its own.

Today, if you must go overboard, do so only with your love-walk, nothing else.

"Let your moderation be known unto all men"
(Philippians 4:9).

The Thief

"The thief comes not but for to steal, kill, and destroy, but I am come that they might have life and that more abundantly" (John 10:10). That verse has long been a dividing line for me. It has clarified issues more than once when something has come into my life that has looked, smelled, tasted or sounded like something other than what my Father says he wants for me.

Just recently, I heard someone say that the thief mentioned in John 10:10 is religion, any system of controls that man puts in place—over others or himself—in order to become worthy of favor with God. My hackles went up when he said it because I'd always been told the thief is Satan. But then he remarked that Satan is behind anything (religion or otherwise) that would keep us from receiving the free gift, so I calmed down.

In thinking about it later, I realized how easy it is for me to fall into religion instead of relationship. Indeed, staying free from the yoke of bondage that comes from performance requires diligence. Oh, how prone I am to wander back to Egypt!

The words a friend spoke at her baptismal service helped me:

"So it is in obedience to what is written in scripture that I am here to be baptized. But I stand here in the hope that it is more than strict obedience: it's an act of love, exemplifying my desire to have a right relationship with God and to surrender my life for him daily. Whilst it is easy to speak those words, to carry them through is a tall order which I can't do in my own strength. None of us can—which is why we have prayer."

An act of love, she said. That's relationship, not religion. Not in her own strength, she said. That's leaning on Jesus, and freedom.

Can there be any question where the abundant life lies?

Today, keep your heart full of love, and keep it free.

"Be sober, be vigilant; because your adversary the devil, as a roaring lion, walketh about, seeking whom he may devour" (1Peter 5:8).

To Do or Not to Do

My favorite scene in the movie *Ten Commandments,* is the one in which we hear Moses' famous command to the children of Israel, "Stand still and see the salvation of the Lord!" In the interest of full disclosure, soon after that incident God asked Moses, "Why are you crying out to me? Tell the people of Israel to go forward!"

Stand still! Go forward! Apparently, there are times when we have to just *stand,* having *done all,* and there are times to go forward—and we have to hear from God to know which is which!

As someone who doesn't like to get wet, I don't fault the Israelites for needing a bit of a push into the sea, even with an army descending on them. But I'll bet the direction to stand still wasn't easy either.

Standing still can sometimes be much more difficult than going forward. There have been a few times I've had to figuratively slap myself and repeat: "Stand still! Just watch!" Sometimes, in the stillness, I see God's hand at work on my behalf. Other times I hear God's instruction—a quiet awareness of what I am to do, or even a thought that comes showing me the next step to take.

So, how do we hear God's voice inside? It began for me when I started to look at the Bible as a truth above the so-called truth of my circumstances. When I saw its directives as wisdom which shouldn't be ignored—or would be to my peril—I began to recognize the still small voice that had been talking to me all along.

In looking back over decades of living, however, I realize my own desires can sometimes muffle what I hear in my heart. Or my fears can drown it out. But I can always rely on the wisdom of the written word. The words between the leather covers of my Bible have never steered me wrong.

Today, listen for his voice as you read.

"I have chosen the way of truth"
(Psalm 199:30a).

Living for Jesus

When I was a child, we sang songs about living for Jesus, but I'm not sure the phrase is even in the Bible. The New Testament does refer to living *through* Jesus, *by* Jesus, *in* Jesus, and *unto* Jesus, or God.

One of our former pastors said that whenever he preached he imagined Jesus standing behind him, listening. He liked to do that because it kept him conscious of whom he was working for. Maybe to "live unto Jesus" is something like that—to live life in such a way that whatever we do can be offered to him, knowing that it would be of value to him because it came from his heart too.

I'm sure there is more to it than that, but that might be a good plumb line.

For example, do I write a blog or a book as an offering to him, or to express my opinions? Or do I love my neighbour as an offering to Jesus because he loves them, or so I'll be well thought of because I'm being nice?

And I wonder if we sometimes find ourselves "living unto" those whose opinion matters most to us, whether it is God, ourselves, our mate, parents, children, friends, or co-workers.

It occurs to me that it is best to live unto someone who loves us best, whose leading is always in green pastures and still waters, and whose words of wisdom or direction are never polluted by ignorance or selfishness, but are founded on truth, justice, love, and perfect knowledge of us and what's going on around us.

There's only one who qualifies for that position.

Today, think about the plumb line.

*"And that he died for all, that they which **live** should not henceforth **live** **unto** themselves, but **unto** him which died for them, and rose again"* (2 Corinthians 5:14-16).

Good Dirt

It's a mystery, really. Oh, I know there are explanations for it, and some people understand it more than others, but to me it's still a mystery that a little plant, thin roots reaching into the earth's soil, can receive nourishment and grow strong—in some soil, at least!

The annuals I planted back in May didn't make it. Well, to tell the truth, they survived but didn't thrive. I guess the clay I put them in (because my husband wasn't around to help me prepare the ground) was too hard for the roots to penetrate and get food. Maybe there's just no nourishment in clay!

So I started over. Off to the garden store I went and came back with new plants and good dirt. And now my pretties are strong, vibrant and beautiful.

Jesus said our hearts are like ground, and our future comes from it. That's a mystery too, but still true. And, strange as it may sound, just like the soil in which I planted my new annuals, our hearts need to be good ground for the seed of God's Word to grow in. We can't fake it. The harvest tells the tale.

Have you ever wondered how we get the kind of heart that's good ground? Wondered whether it is beyond our control or within our reach; perhaps a result of our own diligent work to keep it free from destructive influences?

I have come to the conclusion that knowledge of God's love is the basic necessity of a "good ground" heart—one that brings forth good things. If we have anything to do with it at all, it is to keep focused on the face of Love himself. Only then will we develop a clear heart-picture of how much God loves us. And then, mysteriously, we will be rooted in nourishing soil and grow up, strong and vibrant, into what he has destined us to be.

Today, stay focused on his love.

"For this cause I bow my knees unto the Father of our Lord Jesus Christ, . . .
that ye, being rooted and grounded in love, May be able to comprehend
with all saints what is the breadth, and length, and depth, and height; And
to know the love of Christ, which passeth knowledge, that ye might be filled
with all the fullness of God" (Ephesians 3:14-19).

The Beholder

Have you ever met someone physically beautiful or handsome, but when you got to know them, their good looks faded?

Or have you met someone quite plain, but as you got to know them, they just seemed beautiful?

This phenomenon is no doubt an example of the old adage: Beauty is in the eye of the beholder.

Or perhaps it has more to do with the Biblical truth: "As a man thinketh in his heart, so is he" (Proverbs 23:7).

Apparently, what's on the inside eventually shows up on the outside!

We should always try to look our best. We should maintain our clothes, our hair, our smile, our body, and even check our reflection in a mirror before we go out into the world. Looking our best is never a bad thing.

But our heart needs maintenance as well.

The Bible indicates that God's Word is a mirror which, when we gaze into it over time, actually *changes* us into what we see there.

Today, look into God's Word and see the beauty you were designed to be!

"And let the beauty of the Lord our God be upon us"
(Psalm 90:17).

The Episode

I had an episode that day. I don't have them often since they occur usually sometime before Christmas and again for a day or two when the buds come on the trees in the spring. When it happens I know it's just an episode, but at the same time, strangely enough, I feel like it's all very real.

What happens is that I suddenly think I need a new piece of art to make a room perfect, or a new chair or some other piece of furniture, or—and my husband shudders when this is part of the attack—I think I need to change the color of a room. I drive around all day, running frantically from one store to another, sometimes buying something, bringing it home, bringing it back, and going to the next store on the list, and so on until everything closes down at night. I return things the same day, if I can, to avoid the guilt of hanging on to other people's stuff longer than I should. Or maybe it's just to get that imperfect piece out of my house as soon as possible. Then after a day, or two at most, I get back to normal. My sane perspective returns and I'm happy with the old.

My friend Linda put it in a new light for me one day when she saw my pitiful state. She, apparently, has the same thing happen occasionally. She told me that the last time it happened—quite recently since her great room has been "in reno" for months—she realized she was using the word "need" a lot. "I *need* new carpet; I *need* new lamps; I *need*, I *need*, I *need*," she whined.

Then she watched a show on television where children needed food. She visited a friend in hospital where people needed healing. She noticed a homeless person who needed something—probably something more than a place to spend the night or food, since in our country those things are easy to find.

I got it then. I *need* to recognize how blessed I am, and be thankful. That's what I need.

Today, let's be thankful.

"This I say then, Walk in the Spirit,
and ye shall not fulfil the lust of the flesh" (Galatians 5:15).

Eats, Shoots &Leaves

Author Lynne Truss in her best seller *East, Shoots & Leaves* promotes a "zero tolerance approach to punctuation." She'd turn red in the face if you wrote "boys' hats" if you were referring to one boy's hats!

I absolutely understand Lynne. One of my hot buttons is misuse of words. I don't mean the accidental malapropisms we hear, as when one might say, "That was a ludicrous business deal," instead of, "That was a lucrative business deal." Nor is it when society decides it wants to use a word differently— although that does irritate me. (Remember when "cool" had something to do with temperature?)

My hot button is when Bible translators or paraphrasers, in their attempt to make the scriptures more accessible to modern readers, replace one word with another that has a different meaning, or that changes the original thought of the passage. A case in point: Romans 5:3-5 *" . . . and we glory in tribulations also: knowing that tribulations worketh patience and patience experience and experience hope: and hope maketh not ashamed . . ."*

In my new Bible it says: *" . . . and we glory in tribulations, knowing that tribulation produces perseverance and perseverance, character and character, hope. Now hope does not disappoint . . ."*

The word translated experience in that passage is "DOKIME" which can be translated "proof, testing, or experience". Character isn't mentioned. Even if our perseverance builds our character, it is *God's* good character, his moral excellence, which produces hope in us. What trouble *does* develop is *patience*, if we exercise it, and patience eventually provides *experience* of God's faithfulness and a testimony that shows *God's* character. It is our experience of God's faithfulness in the midst of tribulation—as we are patient and persevere in faith—that produces hope for the future.

Today, don't settle for less than truth.

"Buy the truth, and sell it not; also wisdom, and instruction, and understanding" (Proverbs 23:22-24).

Chicken or Egg

One morning I was looking at an online magazine which advertises books when I found these words: "God allows problems before he sends promises."

I was shocked! It seems to me my Bible is full of promises that cover problems I've not yet encountered. It is God's way.

Cases in point:

- Abraham received promises long before trouble came.
- Joseph received a promise in the form of a dream before he ended up in Egypt.
- David had covenant promises before Goliath showed up.
- Three Hebrew children had promises before they ended up in the furnace: "When thou walkest through the fire . . ." (Isaiah 43:2).
- Paul knew his ministry was to witness to the good news of God's grace, in Rome, before ever a storm tried to get him off course. That God-given purpose included the promise of whatever was needed to complete it.
- Jesus gave you and me warning that in this world we would have tribulation but said we could be of good cheer because he had overcome the world—a promise Paul explains in his letters.

We don't have to wait for his promises. He's already given us thousands.

Today, check out the promises.

"By whom also we have access by faith into this grace wherein we stand, and rejoice in hope of the glory of God" (Romans 5:24).

No Man's Debtor

Many of the Old Covenant laws had to do with repaying what was taken from someone. In fact, the word for "peace" in the Bible, Shalom, means wholeness. When Jewish folk greet each other with the words "Ma sh'lom' cha," they are asking, "How is your peace?" In other words, "Are you whole? Is there something missing that needs replacing?"

It makes sense, then, that it is in God's nature to give back, perhaps in abundance, what is given to him or given to others in his name—even when what you give is time.

When my husband was in a doctoral program in Texas and brought home his first stack of readings, we both were scared! I was even more horrified when I found out it was just one week's reading! When Sunday came, Glenn looked at the box of papers and was sorely tempted to stay home to work his way through it. But he had already decided that he would go to church every Sunday morning. So he did.

Without that one quality decision, made ahead of time and fully committed to, he would have to make the same decision every week, and might spend his student years attending church only sporadically. I don't recall any Sunday when we didn't go to church as a family. And although at one point in the process Glenn was behind everyone in his cohort, he ended up finishing first, several months before the others.

When I was a child I often heard, "God is no man's debtor." The Bible supports it with the sowing and reaping concept found in Corinthians; the "give to the poor and God will repay" promise found in Proverbs; and the "seek the kingdom (God's way of being and doing) first and all these things will be added" admonition in Matthew.

Today, let's ask God to help us be givers-on-purpose—like him.

"Seek ye first the kingdom of God and his righteousness;
and all these things shall be added unto you" (Mathew 6: 32-34).

117

Goodbye and Hello

It was a new year and I was strangely ambivalent about leaving the old one behind. I was glad to leave some of it but, oddly, I was at the same time reluctant to let it go. I couldn't quite put my finger on why. As the year's freshness faded with the return of routine, I realized what was going on.

I had said goodbye to a dear family member in June of that previous year, and as we left the old year behind it felt as if I was saying goodbye to him all over again. And I didn't want to. It felt just as painful as it did the first time.

But there were good things that happened that year—lots of them; I needed to remember and celebrate them. And be grateful.

Being grateful for our blessings is part of the "applying our hearts to wisdom" that is mentioned in Psalm 90, which I read almost every year as New Year's Eve approaches.

Wisdom tells me I don't have to face any of the days ahead without help and strength, and that means I don't have to be afraid of them. Wisdom also says if I'll remember to number my days, I'll use them wisely. It says I'll choose faith and reject fear; I'll appreciate my family and friends, and make sure they know I love them; I'll search the scriptures for direction and hope; I'll enjoy my blessings and share them. And I'll laugh a lot.

When we apply our hearts to wisdom, the "numbering of our days" doesn't depress us, overwhelming us with the speed at which our days go by. Applying our hearts to wisdom brings us to a place of thankfulness that "when it's over," it's not really over, after all. Provision has been made, and the wise heart enjoys the peace and hope it brings.

Live wisely and well today!

"Rejoice evermore. Pray without ceasing. In everything give thanks . . . Prove all things; hold fast that which is good"
(2Thessalonians 5:16-21).

Psalm 19

I've always been intrigued with Psalm 19:7-11.

That's where David talks about the *law* of the Lord, the *testimony* of the Lord, the *statutes* of the Lord, the *commandment* of the Lord, the *fear* of the Lord, and the *judgments* of the Lord.

I remember reading in one of C.S. Lewis' books that he felt those who try to understand the differences between these are on a bit of a fool's errand (my words, not his). In his opinion they are the beautiful expression, in parallel phrases, of the love this poet had for the word of God.

In other words, they are different ways of saying the same thing.

Anyone who knows me will tell you I'm a great fan of Mr. Lewis, but in this I think he was wrong. I think those parallel phrases refer to different things, or at least to different aspects of the same thing.

To know what David is really saying in this psalm will bring more light. And greater light is no fool's quest.

So, dear Jack, we will disagree on this one.

Today, don't be afraid to disagree!

> *"For with thee is the fountain of life: in thy **light** shall we see **light**"*
> (Psalm 36: 8-10).

The Law of the Lord

Just as God created our natural world and included necessary physical laws such as the law of gravity, he established spiritual laws which are just as real.

We are not born knowing the laws of physics, but they are good and they work whether we know them or not. We're better off knowing them because ignorance of them can be detrimental to our well-being. We aren't born knowing spiritual laws either. They, too, are good and work whether we know them or not. We're better off knowing and respecting them because ignorance of them can be detrimental to our well-being and that of people around us.

Some of the laws work in both realms. For example, the law of sowing and reaping—whatsoever a man sows that shall he also reap—is both natural and spiritual. When we think of carrots and cabbages, it's clear the law has nothing to do with reward or punishment. It's just the way things work, naturally. And it's also the way things work, spiritually.

God doesn't punish us with bad harvests if we sow bad seed, any more than he makes us splat on the ground if we jump off a building. It just happens as a result of the law in force. God does, however, give commands to ensure we don't sow and reap bad things. Just one example: "Do unto others as you would have them do unto you."

When we research it, we find out that the laws and the commands connected to them are for our good, always.

This is not meant to suggest that God is not a presently involved father. He didn't just make some laws and send us on our way. The scriptures assure us God is very much in the *present* of our lives. "His eyes are [now] on the righteous and his ears open [now] to their cry" (Psalm 43:15).

But today, love his laws.

> *"The law of the Lord is perfect, converting the soul*
> *[mind, will, and emotion]"* (Psalm 19:7).

The Law of Hair Splitting

Several different Hebrew words have been translated as "law". Some of them refer to the kind of laws I wrote about earlier. They speak of things which are pre-sentenced. Simply, "This is the way this works, so take note and act accordingly." Others refer to directions, decrees, and commands—all of them with specific good purpose. Often it is only in context that we can see their subtle differences.

If this focus seems to be nit-picking, it is—deliberately so. Rightly dividing the word of truth often calls for nit-picking.

Just as in our natural physical lives there are many things that we need to pay attention to minute details of accuracy—Think of a space ship re-entering earth's atmosphere!—so it is in the spiritual.

The words and laws of God, which are spiritual, deserve at least the same degree of attention as do natural laws.

The gospel of Jesus, for which I am eternally grateful, doesn't just give us the good news about our salvation by grace through faith. The gospel also gives us access to a wealth of wisdom often found in the laws referred to previously.

That wisdom is part of what allows us to appropriate the grace-given abundant life that Jesus said he came to give—a life that is here on earth, not just waiting for us in Heaven.

Finding the "gold in them thar' hills" takes deliberate and meticulous effort.

Today, be picky!

"The heart of him that hath understanding seeketh knowledge"
(Proverbs 15:14).

Jesus Shares a Spiritual Law

The disciples were bent out of shape because they couldn't cure the demoniac boy. Jesus' explanation, "It was because of your unbelief. Actually, if you have faith as a grain of mustard seed you could say to this mountain, 'Move!' and it would do it. Nothing would be impossible to you then!"

Can you imagine their reaction to that? Probably much like ours: "*Say what?*"

In Mark 11:23, 24, Jesus talked about that law again, this time in response to Peter's amazement at the death of the cursed fig tree, "I'm telling you, whoever says to a mountain, 'Move!' and doesn't doubt, but believes that what he says will happen, he'll have whatever he says!" Then he gives a specific direction based on that spiritual law: "Therefore [because this is the way things work], whatever things you desire, when you pray, believe that you receive them, and you will!"

Can you see the development?

In Matthew, when talking about the demoniac, he was speaking specifically about them, but in Mark he is talking about whomever. In Matthew he's explaining a *spiritual law*. In Mark he reiterates the law, but then gives a specific application in prayer.

With the disciples, we're gasping for breath! If Jesus hadn't said it, we'd dismiss it as foolishness. But if we believe in Jesus, and in what Jesus says, then we have to do something with it.

If we are praying for something that we already know is his will, then we have the starting point to believe that what we desire when we pray, we will receive.

Today, a little "soul converting" from laws, and "enlightening of the eyes" from commandments can't be a bad thing.

"To give light to them that sit in darkness and in the shadow of death, to guide our feet into the way of peace" (Luke 1:79).

How to Love the Commandments

Ever wondered what to do—what on earth was the next step, or even the right or best thing to do in a particular situation? Perhaps that's what the psalmist was thinking of when he said, "The commandment of the Lord is pure, enlightening the eyes" (Psalm 19:8b).

We have the free will to make our own choices, but Love still gives his commandments: "This is the way to choose. Choose this. This is the way to go. Go here. That is the wrong way. Don't go there."

Love enlightens the eyes.

Not only do we have written commandments to enlighten our eyes in a dark world, we also have the Holy Spirit, sent as Comforter and Guide, who speaks up inside us giving specific commandments just when we need to hear.

And we *will* hear if we are attentive and willing to follow. We will know what to do.

So we can see why the psalmist said the commandment would enlighten the eyes, but why would he call it pure?

If you've lived long at all you know that some of the advice, commands, and directions we receive from others—even some we may ask for—could be impurely motivated. Selfishness, or even malevolence, can be behind them.

But that is never so with God. His commandments are pure. Motivated by his desire for our well-being, they spring from the Father's loving heart.

Today, love the commandments.

"For this is the love of God, that we keep his commandments: and his commandments are not grievous. For whatsoever is born of God overcometh the world: and this is the victory that overcometh the world, even our faith" (1 John 5:2-4).

Need Good Judgments?

In our own justice system, we have laws for the good of all citizens, and judgments for those who don't obey. The judgments are predetermined, although judges have the right to modify them to an extent.

We like to think that most of the judgments brought down in our legal system are good, although sometimes we might consider one too lenient or too severe. We accept, however, that judgments made in our courts might not always be just. Judges can be mistaken, misled, intimidated, or even bought.

Psalm 19:9b says the judgments of the Lord are true and righteous altogether. That word "altogether" is interesting. It's as if the writer wanted to reinforce the thought that there is nothing unrighteous about God's judgments. No mistakes, no shortage of truth, no fear, no selling of favor.

In God's justice system, as well as ours, there has been a prejudgment of actions. However, some judgments are post-event and have preventative intent. For example, when God said to Adam and Eve, "You have to leave the garden," it was because the Tree of Life was there. God didn't want his children to live physically forever in that state of spiritual death, so they had to leave.

I'm glad for that judgment. Can you imagine what a horrible place this earth would be if every evil person we've heard of was still living and active? Would we not cry out for death, our own if not theirs?

God's judgments, in this case and in all others, are most certainly "true and righteous altogether"—sweeter than honey and to be desired more than much fine gold. That thought should help us identify what comes from him and what does not.

Today, be happy for his righteous judgment.

> *"My soul breaketh for the longing that it hath unto*
> *thy judgments at all times"* (Psalm 119:19-21).

Give Me a Testimony

In 1949 a man named Stuart Hamlin was born again at a Billy Graham Crusade in Los Angeles. Shortly after, he wrote and sang the beautiful song "It is no Secret" which became famous in short order. The beginning line of the song went like this, "It is no secret what God can do; what he's done for others he'll do for you."

Some may have thought it was presumptive of Mr. Hamlin to sing those words in front of thousands at Billy Graham's crusades. But they would have been wrong.

Long ago, God gave explicit instructions to the Israelite leaders. They were to tell every new generation of his strength and his works—his stories—so they would hope in him. Those stories were to be treasured, like a valuable heirloom, because they carried the power of hope just as Mr. Hamlyn's song was meant to do.

I just finished, for the second time, Billy Graham's autobiography *Just as I Am*, published about 15 years ago when he was 75. Every night as I put the book on the bedside table, I let out a deep sigh, in awe of the many stories he shared of the faithfulness of God. In every one of them—big stories and little; huge events and small—Dr. Graham's part was twofold and simple, to remain faithful to his calling and look to God for strength, wisdom and favor.

How sad if those stories were not meant to bring us hope, as if God's faithfulness was only for Billy Graham! But, thankfully, that isn't so. Like Jacob's stories to the Israelites, Billy Graham's stories and yours and mine are to be shared with others so the hearers will receive something from them—something wonderful and needful.

Today, let's look for every drop of hope, prophecy, and wisdom that are found in the testimonies of God's goodness.

"the testimony of the LORD is sure,
making wise the simple" (Psalm 19:7).

125

Clean Afraid

Psalm 19 says "the fear of the Lord is clean, enduring forever."

The word "clean" indicates that it is not contaminated, as a cleansed bowl would be clean. There is nothing evil about this fear.

There are two meanings for words translated "fear" from Hebrew or Greek: "respect" and "terror." Respect shows up much more often in reference to God than terror does. When terror shows up it is spoken to those who are doing evil.

We remember that in the old covenant, man's relationship with God was not that of father and child; at best it was friend to friend, but usually God to servant. When Jesus was resurrected, however, he told Mary he was going to "my God and your God, my father and your father."

Perhaps difficult for New Covenant believers to imagine, since that would have been the first time they were told to think of God as their father.

Because of Jesus, our relationship with God can be one in which there is love and honor—the kind that leaves no reason for terror—because we know him to be a good, loving and wise father.

Today, may our fear of God be the kind mentioned here:

*"God is greatly to be feared in the assembly of the saints, and **to be held in reverence** by all those around him. O Lord God of hosts, who is mighty like you? . . . You have a mighty arm; strong is your hand, and high is your right hand . . . . Your faithfulness surrounds you . . . . Righteousness and justice are the foundation of your throne: mercy and truth go before your face. Blessed are the people who know the joyful sound! They walk, O Lord, in the light of your countenance. In your name they rejoice all day long . . . . For you are the glory of their strength"* (Psalm 89).

Tradition

At a beautiful rustic inn one evening in late summer I attended my nephew's wedding. A downpour came to the garden chapel just before the ceremony was to begin, so we waited until the clouds had moved on and the staff had wiped down the seats of the white folding chairs. All in our places, finally, we turned as the music started to see a handsome three-year-old make his way down the aisle, somewhat tentatively carrying a ring on a cushion which he dropped about two feet into his promenade. Then the groom's twelve-year-old niece, led by the bride's faithful dog Bud, made her way to her place at the front, waiting for her cue to read about love from Corinthians 13. Finally, following her one attendant, there was the bride, beautiful and radiant in white, on the arm of her mother. And all the while, whenever the wind blew through the trees and the occasional drop of water fell, a few of us would look up to reassure ourselves that the rain had indeed ended.

As the ceremony continued, the priest who officiated—a French-speaking Robin Williams look-alike—engagingly described the origins of each of the traditions we see in modern weddings. Very enlightening!

As I listened, I thought about our religious traditions and wondered how many we engage in without any understanding of their origin. I wondered how many were intended by God and how many were, instead, introduced by men for reasons that made sense at one time but not anymore.

I confess I'm big on tradition. I believe if a family doesn't have a few, they should make some from scratch. But when it comes to religious traditions, we should find out where they came from, and why. If they didn't originate with our Father, they might just be trouble. That's what Jesus said, anyway.

Today, let's take a second look.

"Full well ye reject the commandment of God that ye may keep your own tradition" (Mark 7:13).

Modern Day Levites

Dr. Terry Teykl, our pastor during our years in Texas, was a guest on the television program *It's a New Day* where he shared about being a "Presence" based church. He talked about the Old Testament Levites and about worship as part of our personal prayer time.

It took me back to the year before we moved to Texas. I was worship leader at a small church and I clearly remember being overwhelmed with the responsibility of leading people to a place of worship.

I knew worship wasn't merely singing hymns or slow, reflective songs. It wasn't limited to singing, or even to words. The job of the worship leader was to help the congregation change where they were looking—to move them from focusing on the world, people, or challenges around them to focusing on God.

But the most important thing I learned about worship back then was that God calls us to worship because *we* need it. As worship brings us into his courts, it connects us to him in some way that is empowering.

Don't misunderstand me: God is always with us. We have his word on that. But as Pastor Terry said, "He wants us to enjoy him as much as he enjoys us." That fellowship happens when we truly worship. And not just in church on Sunday.

Today, for just a while, enjoy Him.

"Oh sing unto the Lord a new song; for he hath done marvellous things: his right hand, and his holy arm, hath gotten him the victory"
(Psalm 98:1).

What Do You Do For Fun?

At a dinner party, a gentleman asked me what I do for fun. I didn't answer right away so he went on to talk about his experiences parasailing and bungee jumping, and from there the conversation expanded to include others who shared similar experiences. I felt a little out of sync since I've never tried any of those and probably never will. Well, I might try parasailing sometime, but never bungee jumping. No, never.

On the drive home I thought about what is fun for me. Snowmobiling, although I haven't done that in ages; skating on a frozen pond, although it's been years since I've done that; swimming with turtles and sailing off Waikiki; dinner with friends; traveling anywhere, at least when I get where I'm going; shopping and lunching and chatting with my daughter; fighting with Casey the cat. There's more, but it's all pretty tame stuff.

At the end of my list—which thankfully was longer than the one I just shared with you—was something that never fails to bring a bubble of joy and raised arm hairs!

I love to see fingerprints! It is just plain, unadulterated fun to see evidence of God's hand at work around me. It's a thrill beyond explanation to witness God-authored coincidences. And to see miracles, things that could never have happened, is exquisite joy. To be part of it in some way, through prayer or giving, or some other way of being God's hands and feet—well, nothing compares. I love to see Heaven touching earth, because I believe we were designed and destined for it, and because I believe it is merely a foretaste of things to come.

From holding a precious child to feeding the hungry—from sky diving to walking on the beach or even winning an Oscar—a rush of pure pleasure accompanies it all. As Paul wrote to Timothy: "God gives us all things richly to enjoy" (1 Timothy 16:11). The joy and pleasures that come from his hand never become old; they never lose their thrill.

Have fun today!

"In thy [God's] presence there is fullness of joy; at thy right hand there are pleasures for evermore" (Psalm 16:11).

Balance

I spent yesterday with about 250 women at the London Women's Directory Spring Conference. The day's theme was "Work Life Balance" and the speakers were women successful in the fields of education, politics, finance, law and business.

Of varying ages and stages of life, some of these women had obviously achieved a good measure of balance, like the business school dean who spends a month in the south of France every year and doesn't check emails on weekends. Some of them, however, were still working on balance, like the law partner, a young mother who falls into bed at 9:00 P.M. after running full tilt since before dawn.

I took home gems of modern wisdom I want to share with you:

- "Be where your hands are. Be present in the moment."
- "You don't *need* it all, and you can't *do* it all. Give yourself a break, regularly."
- "Build a strong support group, one which includes friends, family, and co-workers. And don't forget it's mutual."
- "Manage your self-expectations and self-talk."
- "Occasionally, remind yourself of what's important. Fine-tune that priority list."
- "Don't keep looking back. Where you're going is more important than where you've been."

One recurring thought that shows up on days like yesterday is that life is not a dress rehearsal. I'm not sure what the speakers mean by that, except, perhaps that we don't get do-overs.

So today, here's another gem:

"But let us, who are of the day, be sober, putting on the breastplate of faith and love; and for a helmet, the hope of salvation" (2 Thessalonians 5:8).

ON BEING YOURSELF AND LIVING WITH PEOPLE

All of us were God's idea. Hard to imagine, isn't it?

Daffodils and Roses

When I lived In Victoria, British Columbia, I loved to walk in Beacon Hill Park and enjoy the hosts of daffodils swaying in the breezes that came off the Straits of Juan de Fuca. Another joy—a guilty pleasure because I'd drive out of my way to do it—was to drive down streets lined with Japanese cherry trees loaded with pink blossoms. The peacefulness of either of these scenes would calm me after a day with sixth graders.

But my favorite of that beautiful city's offerings was its many English gardens. Overflowing with myriads of species of flowers, often presided over by the brilliant Tudor rose, the English gardens exploded with colors of every hue.

Recently it was summer camp meeting time at our church. We were enjoying speakers such as Casey Treat, Kate McVeigh, Philip Privete, and Dr. Leroy Thompson. There they were—all of them different in preaching style as well as focus of ministry. While the same in doctrine, no doubt, they might respectfully disagree on some details of the outworking of the gospel.

And there sat all of us, with our various colors and backgrounds, hopes and dreams, challenges and opinions—not one of us "just like the other" as the Sesame Street song went.

I'll bet that even when we all get to be more like Jesus, no one will mistake one of us for the other.

Today, enjoy each other's differences.

"Be of one mind, live in peace; and the God of love and
peace shall be with you" (2 Corinthians 13:14).

Of Flowers and Birds

I'd been reading the manuscript for *Reverend Mother's Daughter,* the autobiography written by Mary Haskett, the founder of our writers group. Even though I'd heard much of her story in bits and pieces over the past years, I still couldn't put the script down.

In the midst of the read, I became impressed with how different we all are, and how different our journeys. And then I thought how very strange it is that on some level we seem to prefer that we all be alike.

How we love to make people over into our own image! How often we flock with birds of our own feather, or try to make ourselves over to look, sound or live like someone else.

How sad that is! After all, we may love daffodils, as I did those that graced Victoria's public parks, but wouldn't a world full of daffodils be rather dull? Maybe, even, a little uncomfortable?

In fact, if I had a dream where there was hundreds of me—or hundreds of you, for that matter!—I'd consider it a nightmare!

I wonder how much better off we'd be if we embraced uniqueness.

Go ahead: Embrace—no, celebrate—your own uniqueness!

Celebrate it all day!

"I will praise thee; for I am fearfully and wonderfully made: marvellous are thy works and that my soul knows right well"
(Psalm 139:14).

Authentic Gospel

Several years ago I received a letter from someone I quoted in my book *Smooth Stones & Promises*. As protocol requires, I had sent the gentleman a copy to show I had quoted exactly what I had requested permission to quote. The letter brought thanks for the book and for the references. It ended with, "We pray you are blessed in your pursuit of an authentic gospel."

That phrase intrigued me: Authentic gospel.

According to Webster's Dictionary:

Authentic: *adj.* real; genuine; worthy of acceptance; original.

Authenticate: *v.* to prove that something is true or genuine.

At first it seemed strange that after 2000 years we'd still have to *pursue* an authentic gospel, but I concluded that pursuit is always connected to the gospel. Have you ever noticed how often we're told to "seek" something—God's face, the kingdom, understanding, wisdom?

Upon further reflection, I realized that the truth-chasing journey on which I invite readers to join me in *Smooth Stones & Promises* is just that—a pursuit of an authentic gospel and a faith-filled lifestyle which will authenticate that gospel to a third-millennium society.

I couldn't help but think of the verse below which speaks of something which is as true, authentic, and acceptable now as it was "from the foundation of the world" (Hebrews 4:3).

Today, let's root out anything fake.

"This is a faithful saying and worthy of all acceptation, that Christ Jesus came into the world to save sinners" (1Timothy 1:15).

What Are You Hiding?

Some time ago, Glenn and I had the opportunity to visit with the president of Power to Change, Leonard Buhler, and his wife, Debbie.

Besides Leonard's obvious passion for Jesus, one thing that stood out about this charismatic man was his belief in the power of the gifts resident within each person, and his obvious love of helping to release them. There should be no wonder that this powerhouse has risen to the position of leadership he holds, and no wonder that the young man who introduced him said, "I'd follow him anywhere."

Later, I watched another gentleman on television, a preacher this time. With great fervour Leon Fontaine of Springs Church in Winnipeg talked about creativity and culture, and specifically about the fact that everyone has gifts, given at birth. One of the few things that make him angry, he said, is a religion that either doesn't recognize the powerful, creative gifts in believers, or that suggests the gifts are only to be used in religious endeavours. He holds that the gifts God gives us are not just so we can serve in church, but so we can shine in our culture.

That reminds me of a comment I once heard. This man said that when he was a young believer he wanted to change the world, but his pastor wanted him to be an usher. That young man later became a very successful pastor who looked at *his* flock as world changers.

Everyone mentioned here has risen to a place of considerable influence, and I expect the reason for it is something my husband talks about in his leadership classes: When you empower others, you don't lose power; you increase it.

Today, open up your hand.

"Give and it shall be given unto you"
(Luke 6:38).

Individuality

It might seem like a contradiction. We prize individuality; yet, we desire community.

In a society that esteems self-reliance, the fact that we need each other might seem to indicate a lack or flaw. We think that if we truly were whole and emotionally healthy we would be able to live and create and love life alone. But that isn't so.

Living as we were designed to live—in relationship—can't be a flawed or substandard existence. In fact, if we place individuality too high in our estimation and work too hard to protect it, we may lose some of the unique design our Creator had in mind when he knit us together in our mother's womb.

Who we were designed to be, as individuals, actually blossoms in community. In fact, our individuality thrives when we live as we were meant to live, in relationship. In some way that may appear contradictory, our true personalities, gifts and callings emerge as we mould ourselves, or allow ourselves to be moulded, to fit into and serve and be served by our community. As we are "knit together" in conformity to that which is good, in family, church and the greater community, our true self—different from all others—is discovered and revealed.

In fact, isn't there something in scripture about when we hold on to something too tightly—even our individuality—for fear of loss, we lose? "There is that withholdeth more than is meet, but it tendeth to poverty" (Proverbs 11:24).

Today, be your unique self and take your special place.

"Now you are the body of Christ and members individually"
(1 Corinthians13:27).

Ripples

Sometimes, when my father would go to the farm, a few of us kids would pile in the back of the truck and go with him to pick berries, swim, or whatever else tickled our fancy for a few hours in that wonderful Newfoundland summer air and sunshine.

If there was not much of a breeze and the water was smooth, we'd be drawn to skipping rocks. We knew our best bet for excelling in this was to find the smoothest, flattest stones and angle the throw just right. Something about a rock skipping effortlessly with four or five landings, creating ripple after ripple in that smooth expanse, brought a joyful sense of accomplishment—of power.

That makes me think about ripples, and the power of making them.

The Bible tells us that life and death are in the power of the tongue. Surely, part of that power is in the ripples one little word can create.

Sometimes words slip out of our mouths. Words of frustration or disappointment, words we don't really want to create harm. Left alone, those words may bring a world of devastation to a relationship—hurt that years won't be able to heal.

Time doesn't heal everything, and unlike the stone's ripples which fade away, ripples made by unkind words can only be stopped by asking for forgiveness.

But good words! They are different. They have life in them, for both the speaker and hearer. The ripples they cause keep going too, and upon every happy remembrance the beautiful waves they created start all over again.

Today, say something life-giving.

"A man hath joy by the answer of his mouth: and a word spoken in due season, how good is it" (Proverbs 15:23).

Let it go!

Someone stole my parking space that evening.

Well, it wasn't really mine. My name wasn't on it, but it was the only one left in the public parking lot by the church downtown across from Cafe One where my husband and I were going to eat. And we always park there.

The spaces slant left, so we drove to the second entrance to drive in properly. As we drove up to the spot, a young girl drove in the first entrance and popped into the spot, pointed *right* by the way, and left us sitting there while she maneuvered back and forth to get into the space.

What to do? What to do? What would Jesus do?

Probably not what we did but, in our defense, we didn't do what I would have liked to do. (*Never mind!*)

Instead, we sat for a minute considering the above, and then drove to another empty space on the cross street. I thought about it later—about the fact that although I've come a long way in these past decades, I still am not where I'd like to be in letting go of little irritations like that.

That night, as I lay in bed mulling it over, I considered *yet again* that if time and practice could remove from our hearts the selfishness and rebellion that turned earth into "death valley" and separated us from the life of God, then Jesus would never have had to die. But it can't, and he had to.

I was *yet again* thankful for the grace that sent Jesus to the cross. Only the love and wisdom of God could come up with such a plan—that we should receive righteousness, and therefore life and blessing, as a gift. All we need to do is believe and receive the gift by faith.

Today let's give some free grace of our own, and "let it go"—whatever it is. After all, Jesus once said,

"Freely you have received, freely give"
(Matthew 10:8).

Power to Forgive

In Capernaum Jesus preached at the house for a while until a commotion above him interrupted his sermon. As the sun broke through he looked up and saw the roof had been uncovered. Watching, perhaps in silence, as four men lowered their friend down on a bed in front of him, Jesus smiled a little.

I know I'm putting my own take on that, but not without reason. The Bible says of Jesus at that moment, "he saw their faith," and since we know faith pleases God, I think he smiled—thrilled by their determination to get help for their friend, delighted that they expected *him* to help. Then, evoking outrage in the already shocked crowd, Jesus—the teacher, healer, lover of sinners—said to the paralytic, "Son, your sins be forgiven you."

The people had seen Jesus heal before and, no doubt, had heard of other miracles like when he made wine out of water, walked on water, and filled up that boat with fish. But *this*! This was too much! *"Your sins be forgiven!"* Not even, "If you change your ways, we'll talk."

"Blasphemous! Only God can forgive sins!" they said.

Jesus shocked them again, "The son of man has power on earth to forgive sins."

Was Jesus just talking about himself, or was he talking about us, too? Think of how very often we are told to forgive: when we stand praying, just as God for Christ's sake has forgiven us, seventy times seven. Listen to the prayer Jesus taught us: "Forgive us our trespasses, as we forgive . . ."

We must have the power. Let's use it. Let's set some people free from their sins against us. If we decide to act on Jesus' words, there will be a lot more freedom in our world. And in us!

Today, set someone free.

"And forgive us our sins;
for we also forgive every one that is indebted to us" (Luke 11:4).

Aeration

That's what they were doing to our lawn—pulling plugs of grass so that the rain could get in and promote good health. As I stood and watched the process for a few minutes, I wondered if that's what forgiveness does for us. Not the forgiveness we receive, but the forgiveness we give. I wondered if anger, frustration, or even disappointment with people closes our hearts, like matted dead grass does the lawn, and forgiveness opens it up again.

I know it's possible to be very angry with some people and still dearly love others. But years of experience has shown me that long held bitterness toward anyone will close my heart toward God eventually.

I have a theory about why it happens. It's found in this verse: "When you've done it unto the least of these my brethren, you've done it unto me" (Mathew 25:40)

When I refuse to forgive—when I've done, said or thought something unlovely to or about someone who has hurt me—my heart knows I've done it to Jesus whether my conscious mind acknowledges it or not. That, then, affects my ability to communicate with him. I feel guilty, so I withdraw. Our relationship begins to change in subtle ways. I don't blame *him* for what my offenders did or said, nor do I secretly want him to punish them and feel disappointed when he doesn't. But I know something has changed between us. I eventually end up at a place where my joy leaks away—my confidence, too. I don't hear God's voice in my heart as clearly as before. I know *he's* not holding out on *me*—his attitude toward me is constant and loving and filled with grace—but something has changed inside me. Something has withered or died.

Maybe that's why asking for and offering forgiveness is such a big deal to Jesus. He wants us to stay vitally connected to him and to be healthy and vibrant, but by refusing to forgive we close our hearts to his life-giving love.

Today, let's let our hearts be free of anything that offends, or clogs up.

"Great peace have they which love thy law:
and nothing shall offend them" (Psalm 119:165).

141

Throwing the Chicken out of the Car

On a warm mid-June day in 2004, my husband dropped me off at Write! Canada, The Word Guild's annual conference held at the Guelph Bible Conference Center. He deposited me and my sleeping bag and luggage on the concrete walk to the dormitory and immediately drove away.

Knowing me well, he had no doubt intuited that I would turn "chicken" as soon as I walked into the gymnasium and saw real writers and authors setting up books and displays and generally looking as if they knew what they were about. Knowing that I would then immediately run home to my safe barnyard, he wisely left me with no recourse but to stay.

I was there because I'd watched a television interview with Christian author Sue Augustine who had advised aspiring writers to "spend time with people who are doing what you want to do." Right after that interview, the station aired an ad for Write! Canada. Now here I was, standing alone in a beautiful, tranquil setting, feeling anything but beautiful and tranquil, and hoping that if I kept a low profile no one would notice I wasn't really one of them.

Even though that first conference was a roller coaster ride of possibilities and impossibilities, after many conferences I still thank God for the immeasurable boon that The Word Guild and Write! Canada, have been to my life. I had started writing a few months before that first conference, but, although I had some idea of what I wanted to do with my precious words, I would not have admitted that I wanted them to grow up and become a book. The conference helped me get over that.

Since then, my association with The Word Guild and its membership has empowered me in ways both practical and spiritual as they have helped me hone my craft, connected me with people from all sides of the publishing industry, and modeled the way a Christian writer stewards the gift. I always take away a bounty.

Today, remember your encouragers and enablers, and be thankful.

"I thank my God upon every remembrance of thee"
(Philippians 1:3).

A Hug in the Mail

One morning I got a hug in the mail.

It came in the form of a self-addressed, stamped envelope from a lady who had been waiting for my book *Keepers of the Testimony* to be released. As a member of the critique group I'm part of, she had already read a couple of chapters. She pre-ordered a copy and sent an envelope, with payment, to make sure she got it "hot off the press."

The envelope felt like a hug because it was a sweet, tangible encouragement that what I had written helped someone in some way—that time spent writing had been well spent. It brought me back to the reason I started writing.

In 2001 and 2002, when I was going through my tussle with cancer, I looked back over my fifty-some years and evaluated my choices, as I imagine most people in that situation might do. I was happy with my path for the most part, but when I asked myself what I *wished* I had done but hadn't, one thing stood out: "I wish I had at least *tried* to write that book."

After months of procrastination, I did try, and found out I loved to write. Since then, many readers have blessed me with their feedback and kind remarks about *Smooth Stones & Promises*. There have been many hugs that have helped propel me forward.

And my friend's self-addressed, stamped envelope was another.

Today, why not give an encouraging "hug" to someone?

*"Therefore, all things whatsoever ye would that men should do unto to you,
do ye even so to them: for this is the law and the prophets"*
(Matthew 7:12).

Rehearsal

Many years ago, as leader in a worship service where several opposing groups had come together to listen to a visiting speaker, I approached the podium with fear and trembling.

In looking out over those who had gathered, I realized that most of them, if not all, loved Jesus. Heartened by that knowledge, I knew that in this one activity—praise and worship—true unity would occur if we would just focus on him.

Recently, one Saturday evening, along with tens of thousands of others, I attended Heaven's Rehearsal at Rogers Centre in Toronto. For more than three hours the centre was filled with music, singing, dance, and readings—praise and worship right out of the book of Psalms. And all of this came from many tribes and races and—even more amazing—denominational backgrounds.

In this much-touted multicultural nation, it was truly miraculous to see representatives of so many cultures come to one place to bless the name of Jesus in unity. It was almost too much for my senses to accommodate and my mind to comprehend.

It was just a rehearsal.

We can barely imagine what the real event will be like.

Today, just think of what true unity might look like.

"But as it is written, Eye hath not seen, nor ear heard, neither have entered into the heart of man, the things which God hath prepared for them that love him" (1 Corinthians 2:8-10).

Fresh like the dew or stuck in the mud?

The pastor in Tulsa spoke on Psalm 133 that morning, his sermon entitled "A Time to Come Together". Not a surprising choice of topic considering the recent hard fought election in his country. His words sounded heartfelt as he shared about how this was a time to pray for the new president-elect and to celebrate with the African American community the incredible breakthrough for which they were so thankful.

As he spoke of the pleasantness of unity among brethren, he said that this scripture was not just referring to brothers in families or in church. In any arena where people need to work together to achieve a common goal, unity will bring the blessedness of fruitfulness, just as the dew of Hermon brings fruitfulness when it descends upon the mountains of Zion and the plains below.

If unity brings fruitfulness, imagine what disunity brings.

To picture it, think of a group of people trying to move a car stuck in the mud. Imagine the owner of the vehicle ignoring the expertise around him, demanding that everyone just do as he says. Think of them arguing for hours about how it should be done. Watch several of them standing back, arms folded, telling the others they will never make it, pointing out every weakness and reminding them of their past mistakes in moving cars.

That morning the pastor talked about how dry and unfruitful the land where people separate themselves from others through criticism and strife. How terrible and how unpleasant it is for brethren to dwell together in disunity.

How much better—whether in a country, church, family, or even in a business project—to recognize that together is better.

Indeed, if unity of spirit isn't achieved, how stuck in the mud is that car!

"Behold, how good and how pleasant it is for brethren
to dwell together in unity" (Psalm 133:1).

Fame and Fortune

Farrah Fawcett, Ed McMahon, and Michael Jackson all died in the same week. Amidst all the related television and internet flurry I found myself conflicted by the coverage of their passing. I certainly wouldn't consider their deaths unimportant, nor the media attention unexpected. It fact, it may be right that we mourn those who have been part of our lives even though we've never met.

Yet, there were many others who died that same week whose names most of us will never know. Mourned by families and friends and others whose lives were touched by theirs, they were soldiers, doctors, teachers, choir members, office managers. There were grandfathers who left us, and grandmothers, mothers and fathers, brothers, sisters, and beloved children. Perhaps life-long friends or friends met only casually, now and then, at the local café or diner. It was the unknowns who died that brought about this entry more than did the three celebrities.

I thought of how many of us might feel celebrity is something worth striving for, as if it carries with it certain happiness. After all, we've seen those smiling, satisfied faces on television, in magazines, on billboards. I wondered if it is only in this era, with its exponential increase in media, that celebrity has become such a sought after prize—a prize which may be a mirage. And I wondered if the unnoticed young couple in the old Ford is just as happy as the paparazzi-swarmed couple in the Jaguar, and the grandparents who spend time with their grandkids at McDonald's just as happy as those who take their grandchildren to exotic destinations.

I'm not saying that the poor are happier than the rich, or that the obscure are better off than the famous. I'm saying that all of us—celebrated publicly or not—are loved and celebrated by someone.

Today, know you are celebrated. Someone has recorded your name.

"Notwithstanding, rejoice not that the spirits are subject unto you, [or that you have become rich and/or successful, as good as that may be] *rejoice that your names are written in Heaven"* (Luke 10:20).

Wealth and Riches

My friend Linda and I met at Starbuck's to collaborate on our monthly critique for Ready Writers London. Before we left, we talked about a plan to shop together for winter coats, because everyone knows one buys better with support and encouragement.

Then I came home to e-mails from friends and family who were taking part in my e-mail "focus group" to help me choose a cover for my book, *Keepers of the Testimony.*

In one of those e-mails, a friend from another province mentioned she'd just got back from spending the afternoon with a mutual friend who is recuperating from a major surgery.

Last night our niece came for dinner and, after working with my husband on his research for a new textbook, hung out on the couch and watched *Bones* with us.

And Glenn just called to say that tomorrow night we're meeting a couple of friends for dinner.

And I began thinking about riches.

Psalm 112:1-3 talks about the blessings of the righteous, and says wealth and riches are in his house.

Even though I love a house filled with beautiful furniture, art, and the latest and best appointments, I think the *best* riches found in any house are love, joy, and peace, and family and friends with whom to share them.

Sometimes, our riches have nothing to do with bank statements or dividends.

Today, count your riches!

> *"He that spared not his own Son, but delivered him up for us all,*
> *how shall he not with him also freely give us all things?"*
> (Romans 8:32).

Love Never Fails

I was off to Newfoundland, where I was born and raised.

The occasion was my mother's 90th birthday party. Some of the grandchildren who live thousands of miles away weren't able to attend the afternoon tea celebration, but they sent greetings to be read on the day.

In my daughter's note, I was touched to read about my mother's legacy to her. Gillian shared about how when she was a child she looked forward to the smells in Nanny's house—the sweet fragrance of cookies coming out of the oven, bread just baked, or jams boiling on the stove—and the ever present promise of chocolate treats in the blue dish on the end table in the living room. Nanny was always ready for her visit.

Gillian wrote that the biggest part of what she loved about those trips was the faithful assurance "that there would be you, Nanny, making sure that everyone was fed, happy, healthy, and well taken care of." Now, whenever Gillian enters a bakery or a home where someone has been "cooking good food," it evokes the memories of sweet smells on Sparkes Lane, and she remembers the faithfulness of love. Now, as an adult, her understanding of the unfathomable, unearned love of God is strengthened by her memories of her grandmother's love and faithfulness.

Maybe it is always the case that our first experience of—and impression of—God is found in the lives of his people. We are, after all, made in his image. Perhaps that is why the Bible, so often, tells us to love.

Our love is to be unfeigned; the kind that forgives seventy times seven, that puts the beloved's welfare above one's own, that seeks the good of the beloved at all times. In short, the kind of love that died for us.

Today, let's let the love of God that's been shed abroad *in* us, out!

> *"Whether there are prophecies, they will fail . . .*
> *tongues will cease . . . knowledge will vanish away . . .*
> *love never fails"* (1 Corinthians 13:8).

Therefore

Jesus was finishing up his famous Sermon on the Mount and, in the beginning of Matthew, Chapter 7, was talking about a subject I don't much like: Judging others.

I don't like the subject, not because I hate judging but because I've always felt I'm good at it. In my defense—and I'm sure by now I need defending—later in that same book there is indication that we *should* judge: "Beware of false prophets! . . . By their fruits you will know them!" and "Do not give what is holy to the dogs."

Now tell me, doesn't that sound like judging to you? Judging who is false and who won't appreciate what is holy?

So what is going on here?

You'll probably agree that we have to judge occasionally. Wisdom and prudence requires it. So what kind of judging are we not to do?

This morning, the "therefore" in Matthew 7:12 helped me get a little brighter light on it. It comes after the judging comments. Jesus is talking about asking, seeking and knocking, and about the fact that God gives good things to those who ask. Then, connecting that to what comes next, he says, "*Therefore*, whatever you want men to do to you, do also to them, for this is the law and the prophets."

Apparently, there's a reason why, even though I am to judge right from wrong, safe from unsafe, and false from true, I am to *do unto them*—the wrong, unsafe, and false—as I would have them do unto me. I am to give them grace when I see their failings, pray for them when I see they're off track, tell them when they're in danger, and love them no matter what, because Jesus loves them and I love Jesus.

Today, try this:

"Be the children of your Father in Heaven: for he maketh his sun to rise on the evil and on the good, and sendeth rain on the just and on the unjust"
(Matthew 5:45).

Criticism

Someone asked me if my husband took criticism well. I laughed before I could stop myself, remembering how well he had taken my unspoken criticism the previous night when we had arrived at a hotel and found we had no reservation.

The truth is that we were both pretty cranky, having already been delayed an hour by construction on the highway and now another 20 minutes while the desk clerk—even though he had a room available—tried to figure out why we had no reservation. Of course, I asked Glenn if he had the confirmation number. He didn't, and—I couldn't help myself—I sighed noticeably. Of course, he wasn't impressed with that, and before long—well, you can imagine.

After we calmed down a few minutes later, I realized I couldn't in good conscience judge my husband for his lack of grace in the face of my impatient sigh, at least not with my long and short term memory still intact. After all, I've been known to have my own issues with accepting criticism.

Like when I was writing my first book. Glenn read the first draft and suggested that I should tell a little bit about what was going on in my life at the time frame of the book's beginning. I didn't want to do that. Later, a well-published author who critiqued that first chapter at Write! Canada told me the same thing. *Silly man,* I thought! Then, at the same conference, an editor from a well-known publishing house told me, "Start with a story." So I drove home thinking they were all idiots, and then left the manuscript alone for three weeks before I decided, "Maybe I'll try."

Do we all hate it when our critics are right? Eventually I do try to look at most of them as carriers of God's grace—Really, I do!—because sometimes he sends help before I know I need it.

But then again, sometimes my critics are just having a bad day. Maybe someone criticized them.

Today, love on your critics a little bit.

"Iron sharpeneth iron"
(Proverbs 27:17).

Passages

One day I had lunch with a young woman who had just secured a great new job and would be moving into her own apartment the following month. She told me her mother had enough furniture to fill the new place and was at first going to try to add it to another shipment from down east. But then a new plan emerged: Mother/Daughter Road Trip in a U-Haul!

Having done my own U-Haul trip to Texas for my husband's studies, I shuddered at the thought.

But this trip would be less about furniture than it was about a rite of passage for her and her mother. For her mother, this was about seeing one's child setting out on her own life's journey. Different from that first leaving home for university, since children almost always come home from school, this "setting out" says she's an adult and will have her own home from now on.

2 Corinthians 3:18 says we go from glory to glory. Perhaps this scripture is referring to something else—something more mystical—but I think it applies here as well.

Every stage of life has its own glory, its own joy, and to fully experience the journey is a gift from God.

I remember how glorious it was to watch our daughter grow into a beautiful, responsible adult with her own glory-road ahead of her. I know, too, how precious a gift it was to share the experience of that road's beginning!

Today, share someone's journey and their joy.

"Whensoever I take my journey into Spain, I will come to you: for I trust to see you in my journey and to be brought on my way thitherward by you, if first I be somewhat filled with your company" (Romans 15:23-25).

The Witness

My friend Ruth, author of two novels based on true life stories, *Not Easily Broken* and *Not Far From The Tree*, recently participated in book signings in retirement homes throughout Southern Ontario. She came back to our writers' group with stories—some poignant; some delightful.

Her experiences there made me wonder how many mothers, fathers, aunts, uncles, and family friends sit in retirement homes feeling "unseen" by the very people they poured their lives into.

I thought of my own mother who loved the attention showered on her when our family celebrated her 90th birthday with an open house and family dinner. I remembered how pleased she was to see not only her children but also friends, cousins, nephews and nieces and great-granddaughters. How reluctant she was to have the day end!

After the time my friend spent in those retirement homes, really seeing the people, she asked if she could take a few copies of my book, *Keepers of the Testimony*, with her next time. She wanted those elderly men and women to know what a gift they have to give in the stories they can tell.

She wanted them to know that they still bring value, that they can yet be seen.

Today, let's let someone know they have a witness.

"And she called the name of the LORD that spake unto her,
Thou God seest me" (Genesis 16:12-14).

Rejoice with Those that Rejoice

About 8:00 P.M. one evening I got a call from my friend Linda. She was laughing and talking so loudly that at first I had difficulty recognizing who it was or what she was saying.

Then I caught it.

"I'm published!! I'm published! Can you believe it? I'm published!"

I squealed too.

Linda had just received word that her first article was accepted for publication in *Beyond Ordinary Living*, a new Canadian magazine. She called me as soon as she got the news, even though she was on her way out with her husband.

Months earlier, I had encouraged Linda to start writing, and she knew I'd be thrilled about her first publication. She wanted to share her joy with me right away. And I did—share the joy that is. I was so excited! Even though I'd already had a piece rejected by the same magazine.

The Bible's admonition to rejoice with those that rejoice apparently has two benefits. The original "rejoicer" increases by sharing, and the rest of us get in on the good feelings.

Today, find someone to rejoice with, and see how good it feels.

"And when he cometh home, he calls together his friends and neighbors and says to them, Rejoice with me; for I have found my sheep which was lost"
(Luke 15:6).

A Visit with Pastor

All that week Dr. Terry Teykl, from Houston, Texas, was a guest on the television program *It's a New Day* on Vision TV.

He was talking about prayer—his passion for years—and in listening to him I was brought back to our years in College Station where he was our pastor at Aldersgate United Methodist Church.

Terry's ministry to our family while we lived in Texas was a gift from God. His quirky, dry sense of humor and his ability to encourage us and point us to Jesus every week, with just about twenty minutes' pulpit time, picked us up during some very difficult times.

The church was somewhat more formal than I was used to. One Sunday, early in our time there, I felt I wanted to go to another church, one closer to my own tradition. At my request, we drove to another church.

When we got to the parking lot, we sat in the car for a moment. Then I said to my husband, "Could we go back to Aldersgate? I think I need to listen to Terry this morning."

It wasn't really Terry I needed. It was the way he turned my eyes to Jesus that I needed that day, and I knew it.

We didn't ever go hunting for a new church again.

Today, think about those who have been God's gift to you.

"And I beseech you brethren to know those who labour among you . . .
and esteem them very highly in love for the work's sake"
(1 Thessalonians 5:12-13).

"Look at me!"

I imagine every parent has heard, "Mommy, Daddy, look at me! See what I can do!" more times than they can count. While it may seem an egocentric perspective, we happily indulge it in little ones, especially our own little ones.

A while ago, my son-in-law, Ryan, was part of a group that produced a fund-raising video for a missionary organization that builds schools in South America. In the video, a man who lived in one of the villages where a school had been built was being interviewed. He said with gratitude, "You looked at us and you saw us." His words brought tears to my eyes. They told me that many had looked but had not seen. I wondered how often many of us, in our affluent culture, look but don't see, and how often we, ourselves, feel unseen.

The need to have a witness to our lives is something which is born in us. Nothing to be ashamed of, it is almost cellular, or molecular, no doubt put there by our Creator. Maybe so we would always *feel* the need for each other, because we *do*, in fact, need each other.

There's a well-worn phrase, "As God is my witness!" In fact, God is our most attentive witness. Even when we feel there is no one else who cares to witness our triumphs, failures, troubles or joys, we can be assured God does. And he doesn't just look. He sees and responds when we call. 2 Chronicles 16:9 tells us about it: "The eyes of the Lord run throughout the whole earth, to show himself strong on behalf of those whose heart is loyal to Him."

We have a witness—of that there can be no doubt. There are many other references to how lovingly watchful God is. Just get a concordance and follow his eyes.

But still, he calls us to *be* witnesses, asking us to weep with those that weep, rejoice with those that rejoice, and to freely meet needs when we can, even if it is just the need to be seen.

Today, look and see.

"The eyes of the Lord are on the righteous and
His ears are open to their cry" (1 Peter 3:12).

The Visit

One day when I visited my mother in the retirement home, she informed me my childhood pastor would like to see me. I found him in the activity room where we had a lovely visit, chatting about my new book which he had just read and which was the reason for his invitation.

I was inordinately pleased with his kind words about the book, perhaps because I remembered him as the model of what a good pastor might be. He always carried himself with the calm and gentle demeanour that I imagined Jesus had. He seemed strong and confident in his faith, focused more on God than on his vocation. He handled the word of God with integrity. And he treated his sheep with respect, even the little ones—he always used our names when he spoke to us.

If I sound obsessed about the "name" thing, it may be because I am, a little. Maybe it has something to do with wanting the "witness" I wrote about earlier. Or perhaps it's because when I was a child my pastor seemed to represent Jesus and—as crazy or narcissistic as it may sound—my pastor's willingness to focus attention on me, even briefly, told the "child me" that I wasn't just a nameless face to an unapproachable and impersonal God.

I am still thankful for this pastor who imprinted juvenile Fay with the confidence that God, too, knew her name.

Today, think about the One who knew you before you got here.

"And of Zion it shall be said, This and that man was born in her: and the highest himself shall establish her. The LORD shall count, when he writeth up the people, that this man was born there."
(Psalm 87:5-6).

A Mystery

Many years ago at my nephew's wedding, the bride and groom danced to the song "Walk Through this World with Me." As I glanced around the room at the affectionate smiles of family members looking on as they danced, I thought about what a blessing it was to have such people with whom to walk through my world.

My husband and I have moved several times over almost four decades. I have met new friends in our neighborhoods, work places, and churches—many of whom have become like family, embedded in my life. Even though with subsequent moves I rarely some of see them, they are still somehow part of my life even though they are not actually in my day to day world.

It seems both strange and natural that, in the same way, dear ones who have moved to Heaven—my father, my sister, and my nephew—are still, and always will be, in my life. Our family and friends will never be removed from that span of time, that "walk through the world," that is ours, even if they leave it before us.

It's a mystery, really.

C.S. Lewis talked about it in reference to his wife, Joy. After she passed away he said that whenever he could stop *trying* to keep her close, she just naturally *seemed* even closer to him than when she was still here.

Some things simply defy reason. How foolish we are to demand that empirical evidence be available to establish all truth when we live with mysteries every day.

Today, think about another mystery Jesus talked to his Father about:

"Neither pray I for these alone, but for all who shall believe on me through their words, that they all may be one; as thou, Father, art in me, and I in Thee, that they also may be one in us, that the world may believe that Thou hast sent me" (John 17:20-21).

Out with the Old

I'm getting a new desk today.

I remember the day we got the old one in the fall of 1977. Glenn and I had just moved into our first house on Vancouver Island. Billed as "California style," the house nestled among tall trees on a hill just back from the road that led to the picturesque town of Sooke.

Our wooded hill was home to a few deer that grazed outside our bedroom window almost every morning. The oak desk would have settled nicely in front of the window that looked out on that hill, instead of in the third bedroom with the window that looked out on the house next door. But there were no computers or internet in those days, writing was far from my mind, and the desk was more for storage of bills and other paperwork than anything else. So it stayed in the room without the view.

The old desk is holding up pretty well after three decades, nine moves, and thousands of miles. It still looks pretty decent, although slightly stained by something I left sitting on it years ago. Even though the finish has worn away right in front of the keyboard and the drawers are difficult to move, I'm reluctant to let it go.

Here's the thing: my desk and I have a long history together. That's why, instead of bumping it to the curb for the trash man or selling it to a student looking for temporary furniture, I'm going to keep it. It will be a great place to keep the old paperwork my husband insists we hold on to. And I'll get to visit it and its stories once in a while.

I like to keep my friends, too. Even if worn and damaged with time and misuse, friends are well worth keeping, even more so than my memory-laden desk.

Today, call an old friend.

"Thine own friend, and thy father's friend, forsake not"
(Proverbs 27:10).

ON CLOCKS AND CALENDARS

Are we there yet?

Are we there yet?

Hurry Up and Wait

Why do we hate to wait?

We rush to grow up, get married, make money, buy a house, spend money, change locations—make decisions.

To those of us who are chronically in a hurry, waiting can be an extremely dangerous occupation.

Waiting, Fay? Don't you mean rushing?

No, I mean waiting. While we're waiting for something to happen, whether good or bad, we feel *so* much pressure to act that the resulting stress feels unbearable. We may not know exactly what to do, but we think we should do something! We think anything would be better than waiting.

And therein is the danger: Doing *something* is not always better than doing nothing. Doing the wrong thing can be devastating! It can take us off the right path, or shut us down just before a breakthrough.

Sometimes the only "doing" required is waiting, whether it is for God to work, for nature to take its course, or to know what our next move should be.

Some of the best things in life can't happen without the passing of time. Perhaps that's why we're told to let "patience have her perfect work."

The "work" of patience is to hold us firm until we lack nothing, until what God has spoken is fulfilled.

Time and waiting are often our friends. Patience always is.

> *"In your patience possess ye your souls"*
> (Luke 21:19).

My Trees Talked

I was in the kitchen cleaning up from breakfast when I looked up and glanced out the windows across the room. There, I saw three tall, beautiful, perfectly shaped trees—their branches already draped in white—standing elegantly and peacefully as the first snow of the season fell around and on them.

Suddenly and surprisingly, the sight of them gave me great pleasure. I remembered the mess of dirt that was our backyard when we moved here in 2001. I could hardly wait for the landscape contractor to plant grass and trees. Although part of me wanted to see fully grown trees planted right away, another part hoped they wouldn't do it that way. Our family had moved around quite a bit, and although we had trees on the lawns of several of the houses we lived in, I had often said to my husband, "Someday, we're going to stay somewhere long enough to actually watch trees grow."

Of course, the trees were always growing, but not so I could notice. So now, in this place, I wanted to start small. Sure enough, I came home one day to find three little not-much-more-than-saplings standing tentatively and looking lonely in their new environment.

Years have passed since then, and as I enjoyed my tall, full trees that winter morning, I felt as if I had reached a long-awaited milestone—and with very little effort, except a good watering on hot days and a willingness to stay put! Not only did the calm beauty of my trees warm my heart on a cold winter day, they spoke to me as well, "See! Here we are! We didn't appear overnight but we're here! And you got to watch us grow. Patience always has her perfect work."

Smart trees! They reminded me that the other things I want to see in my life, and within myself, that are not growing up as fast as I'd like, just need patience. In due season, I will reap, if I faint not.

Today, don't give up.

"If we hope for that we see not, then do we with patience wait for it"
(Romans 8:25).

Patience

Remember when Doris Day sang so convincingly, "Whatever will be, will be," smiling brightly as she did? I thought of her the other day when I was reading the first chapter of the book of James. It occurred to me that in every trial of faith there is an accompanying temptation: to accept a "que sera, sera" attitude.

In other words, there is a temptation to stop expecting God to fulfill his promises—in this particular situation, at least.

The book of James lets us know we don't have to do that. In fact, it implies we mustn't do it because patience has a work to do in the midst of every trial.

Jesus, too, told us about the work of patience. In talking about the seed of the word, he said that it is *with patience* that we bring forth the fruit, or harvest, which comes from the word, and that without it, no fruit will be brought to perfection.

But here's the thing about patience: We have to put it to work.

If the beautiful and talented Doris meant to suggest we have no influence over our future, she was wrong. Our destiny waits on our choices, and one of the choices we need to make is to put patience to work.

Here's what patience does: It waits with expectancy, works with diligence if that is what is called for, looks eagerly for the fruit of the word, and keeps smiling in the interim.

Today, we can be patient. Really, we can.

"But that [which fell] on the good ground are they,
which in an honest and good heart, having heard the word, keep it,
and bring forth fruit with patience" (Luke 8:15).

Fruit takes Time

It was a long hot summer, my days moving as slow as the season. Every evening at dinner on the patio, my husband and I watched the sun set slowly, and it seemed the days themselves were reluctant to end—as if time itself wanted to stand still.

But time showed its true blazing colors late that summer when I went to a convention in Fort Worth, Texas, with a friend from years ago. We had a lovely time together recalling events of the past and catching up on our and our children's lives.

My daughter joined us part of the way through the week. As I thought of how young Gillian was the first time we went to the conference and how I had been just a few years older than she is now, it all came together to make me somewhat nostalgic. I wanted my youth back—my old friends, my little girl. Time had gone too fast!

Then my former student, "Jamie" in my book *Keepers of the Testimony*, drove up from Austin to visit. As I waited for him in the lobby of the hotel, my eyes examined every twenty-something young man who walked in. And then there he was, striding toward me with a smile that brought me back to 1994. As the four of us visited over lunch and then had a quiet prayer time in the sitting area far enough from the third floor pool to give privacy, I made my peace with time. As I thought about how much had transpired in his life over the years, I was so thankful for where he is right now. God has brought him "through it all" to a good place.

And then I saw it. Just as fruit must ripen or it doesn't reach its potential, the passing of time is necessary for bringing the fruit of righteousness to maturity. And children must not remain children, and we must embrace growing older. Time is a vehicle by which God releases us into our destiny, and every stage of our destiny has its own glory, its own purpose and delight.

Today, let's recognize the glory that surrounds us.

"Surely goodness and mercy shall follow me all the days of my life, and I will dwell in the house of the Lord forever" (Psalm 23:6).

Only with Age

It was my birthday and, as I have done every year for a decade or more, I thought of a young woman with whom I share my birthday. On that particular birthday, Aislinn was half my age. A young mother of two, she was still in her twenties for one more year.

Having watched Aislinn grow up in church and school, I'm confident that she has a heritage of faith and a good foundation for life. Still, every year on our birthday my wish for her is this understanding:

- That seeds sown *will* grow into beautiful fruit if we care for it.
- That people are precious, and family and friends are our true wealth.
- That the stories lived by the generation who got here before us hold gems of wisdom we can mine.

But some things can only be learned with age and experience, for it is only with age that we receive the benefits of watching seasons come and go. So I pray that she finds through life experience that God really is faithful.

Today, be thankful for your years. Use them to bless the next generation.

"Those who are planted in the house of the Lord shall flourish in the courts of our God. They shall still bear fruit in old age. They shall be fresh and flourishing to declare that the Lord is upright; he is my rock, and there is no unrighteousness in Him" (Psalm 92:12-15).

Marathons and Finish Lines

That Sunday my husband ran his first half marathon.

I watched him, fresh and hopeful, leave with the crowd as I headed off to Starbucks to sit and drink coffee while reading my brand new copy of *Yours, Jack* (a gift from my hubby who knows I'm a huge fan of C.S. Lewis).

Ninety minutes later, even though Glenn had told me he wouldn't be there for another hour, I headed back to the finish line, just in case. I was totally unprepared for my reaction upon seeing the runners come in.

Here they came, sometimes one by one, sometimes in small groups. Children hobbling with parents holding their hands, one girl bursting into tears just feet from the finish line, a senior gentleman flanked by two young men who encouraged him to keep going, and some—like my hubby—still powerful to the end.

I wept!

I thought of how those who have gone before us to Heaven must peer with outstretched necks to see loved ones round that last bend. I thought of my father—weak when he left here at 90 after a good, strong life—and how he must have thrown back his head and laughed out loud with joy to see the beautiful shore.

And I thought of how precious in the eyes of the Lord the homecoming of his saints must be.

And I was undone.

Today, think about all that is to come.

> *"Thou shalt guide me with thy counsel,*
> *and afterward receive me to glory"* (Psalm 73:24).

ABOUT THE AUTHOR

Fay Rowe grew up on the east coast of Canada where she attended university at Memorial University of Newfoundland and earned degrees in Education and English. She has taught in both private and public schools in several cities in Canada as well as in College Station, Texas.

As a teacher of fourth graders and junior high students, and in settings such as Sunday morning service, Wednesday night Bible study, and various Women's Club and conference events, Fay has shared powerful insights with people of all ages.

In her books, Fay encourages her readers' faith while challenging them to walk ever closer to Jesus. Her second book, *Keepers of the Testimony,* won a TWG (The Word Guild) Award (Relationships Category) in 2009. She is now blogging, working on her first novel, and producing a weekly podcast.

Mother of a grown daughter, Gillian, and mother-in-law of Ryan, Fay lives in Southern Ontario with her husband, Glenn.

Fay's website:
www.fayrowe.com

ABOUT THE BOOKS

"*Keepers of the Testimony* is instructive, inspiring, and exquisitely written. An excellent book, it has one of the best opening chapters I have read in a long time. I love the sound biblical foundation incorporated, with lots of scripture actually quoted. Fay Rowe has the gift of being able to tell her stories with both humor and humility. She keeps them God-centered so that there is no sense of ego in them." Karen Henein, Lawyer, Speaker, Author, *Counsel of the Most High*, *Bent Out of Shape*, and *Seeking the Truth About Money*

"*Smooth Stones and Promises* [Formerly *What's In A Name*] is a profound, well documented piece, equal in both its scholarly and spiritual merits. 'Dog ears' are used to highlight pages on which I paused for breath because of the profundity of what I was reading." Dr. Norel London, Professor Emeritus, University of Western Ontario, Excerpt from letter, used with permission.

"A wonderfully uplifting read, *Keepers of the Testimony* stirred in me the desire to once again share my own testimony." Mary Haskett, Author, *Reverend Mother's Daughter* and *Because We Prayed*

"*Smooth Stones and Promises* is a book every Christian must read." Donna Fawcett, Author of Donna Dawson novels *Redeemed, Adam and Eve Project, Vengeance,* and *Rescued*